CULTURES OF THE WORLD
ARGENTINA

by Ethel Caro Gofen/Leslie Jermyn

BENCHMARK BOOKS

MARSHALL CAVENDISH
NEW YORK

PICTURE CREDITS
Cover photo: Viesti Associates, Inc. © R. & M. Magruder
Bettman Archives: 23, 24, 96, 105, 109 • Victor Englebert: 12, 19, 40, 57, 58, 63, 71, 84, 88, 101 • Focus Team
Photo Agency: 48, 50, 102 • Getty Images/Hulton Archive: 34 • Eduardo Gil: 4, 5, 7, 9, 13, 16, 19, 22, 27, 30,
31, 37, 38, 39, 41, 43, 47, 53, 54, 55, 56, 58, 60, 61, 62 (both), 64, 66, 67, 69, 70, 72 (both), 78 (both), 80, 82,
85, 87, 90, 92 (both), 93, 94, 95, 97 (both), 98, 99, 100, 103, 112, 113, 114, 117, 120, 121, 122, 123, 124, 125,
127, 128 • Hans Hayden: 46, 76 • HBL Network Photo Agency: 44, 45 • Hulton Deutsch: 20 • The Hutchison
Library: 3, 6, 11, 14, 29, 42, 67, 68, 110 • The Image Bank: 32 • John Maier, Jr.: 83, 104, 106 • North Wind
Pictures: 21 • Tony Perrottet: 12, 26, 33, 57, 64, 65, 73, 75, 91, 107, 116 • Secretaría de Turismo, Argentina: 18
• David Simson: 1, 36 • South American Pictures: 8, 10, 15, 17, 25, 28, 40, 49, 51, 52, 68, 74, 77, 86, 100, 115,
118, 125, 129 • Liba Taylor Photography: 74 • Times Media Private Limited: 130, 131, 135 (both)

ACKNOWLEDGMENTS
With thanks to Virginia Tuma, Ph.D. candidate in Literature, Duke University,
for her expert reading of the manuscript.

PRECEDING PAGE
Argentine "cowboys" show off their bravery at a rodeo.

Marshall Cavendish Corporation
99 White Plains Road
Tarrytown, NY 10591
Website: www.marshallcavendish.com

© 1990, 2002 by Times Media Private Limited
All rights reserved. First edition 1990.
Second edition 2002.

Originated and designed by
Times Books International, an imprint of
Times Media Private Limited, a member of the
Times Publishing Group

Printed in Malaysia

Library of Congress Cataloging-in-Publication Data:
Gofen, Ethel, [date]
    Argentina / by Ethel Caro Gofen, Leslie Jermyn.—2nd ed.
      p. cm.—(Cultures of the world)
    Includes bibliographical references and index.
    Summary: Presents the history, geography, government, economy, people,
and social life and customs of Argentina, the eighth largest country in the world.
    ISBN 0-7614-1358-8
    1. Argentina—Juvenile literature. [1. Argentina.] I. Jermyn, Leslie. II. Title.
III. Series.
F2808.2.G64 2002
982—dc21   2001047759

6 5 4 3

CONTENTS

Argentina is blessed with a beautiful countryside, friendly people and a colorful culture.

Argentina is a land of legendary heroes—one of South America's most prominent liberators, José de San Martín, was born in Argentina.

INTRODUCTION

ARGENTINA IS A COUNTRY of endless plains, caped cowboys, and irresistible music. Located in the southeastern corner of the South American continent, Argentina is a distinctly South American country, yet the country has much in common with Europe and the United States. Argentina is a place that thousands of European migrants have come to call home and a country where Spanish is sometimes spoken with an Italian accent. Descendants of Welsh shepherds live in the far south of the country, while indigenous peoples still inhabit northern areas. Argentina has its own brand of the cowboy, the *gaucho* ("GOW-choh"), and an illustrious tradition of sports, arts, and culture. The country has produced one of the greatest soccer players of all time, Diego Armando Maradona; one of the century's most renowned writers, Jorge Luis Borges; and one of the world's most passionate dance forms, the tango. Today, Argentines are deservedly proud of their country—with its colorful history and unique peoples.

GEOGRAPHY

WHETHER YOU DREAM of mountain peaks, sandy beaches, or fertile plains, Argentina has them all. This vast South American country stretches about 2,300 miles (3,700 km) long and has a dramatically diverse climate, ranging from subtropical in the north to sub-Antarctic in the south. Since Argentina lies in the Southern Hemisphere, the climate is hottest in the north, near the equator, and coldest in the south.

Argentina is the eighth largest country in the world and the second largest country in South America, after Brazil. Argentina's land mass covers almost 1.1 million square miles (2.8 million square km) and measures 868 miles (1,397 km) across at its broadest point.

Argentina's neighbors are Bolivia and Paraguay to the north, Brazil and Uruguay to the east, and Chile to the south and west. The Atlantic Ocean on the east and south and the Andes Mountains to the west form long natural borders.

Argentines are proud of their country's great natural beauty. Featuring long stretches of snowcapped mountains and miles of seashore, Argentina boasts remarkable extremes of elevation. The Salinas Chicas, or Small Salt Mines, is the lowest place on the South American continent—131 feet (40 m) below sea level. Near the Chilean border, the summit of Mt. Aconcagua, an extinct volcano, is the highest peak in the Western Hemisphere—22,834 feet (6,960 m) high.

7

THE NORTHERN LOWLANDS

Northern Argentina consists of heavily forested lowlands. Early settlers called one area in this region the Gran Chaco, or hunting ground, to distinguish it from the *pampas* ("PAHM-pahs"), a vast cattle-grazing region farther south.

Few people live in the forests of the Chaco. The region is rich in forest products, but its fertility is limited in some parts by swamps and in other parts by periodic drought. Winters are dry, while summers are hot and humid, with temperatures rising as high as 104°F (40°C).

Another area in the northern lowlands is called Mesopotamia, and it includes the provinces of Entre Ríos, Corrientes, and Misiones. Mesopotamia and Entre Ríos both mean "between rivers." This area lies between the Paraná and Uruguay rivers. Rolling grassy plains, rivers, and swamps are the chief features. The climate is warm and wet all year round. Ranchers raise cattle, horses, and sheep; farmers grow flax, wheat, and fruits.

The Misiones province in north-eastern Mesopotamia has heavy rainfall and thick forests. The spectacular Iguazú Falls on the Brazilian border are also located here. The region's most famous crop is the holly plant, used to make *yerba mate* ("ZHER-bah MAH-teh"). This brewed herbal tea, the *gaucho*'s favorite drink, is served all over Argentina.

Palm trees grow in savannahs on the wet and swampy lowlands of Entre Ríos.

IGUAZÚ FALLS: A WORLD-CLASS TOURIST DESTINATION

Misiones, in northeastern Mesopotamia, boasts many spectacular waterfalls; the impressive Iguazú Falls on the Brazilian border is the most awesome of them all. Álvar Núñez Cabeza de Vaca, a Spaniard explored this gorgeous cascade in 1541.

Iguazú is a Guaraní Indian word meaning "great water." More than 275 waterfalls surround an 8,100-foot (2,469-m)-wide arc in the Iguazú River. These waterfalls plunge roughly 270 feet (82 m) over a series of small islets, creating spectacular sprays and rainbows. The largest waterfall, called Devil's Throat, is more than 350 feet (107 m) high.

A Brazilian army officer, Edmundo de Barros, conceived the idea of creating a nature reserve around the waterfalls in 1897. Two separate parks were established by the Argentine and Brazilian governments. The Argentine national park covers 132,500 acres (53,623 hectares) of tropical jungle. A wildlife reserve shelters hundreds of species of birds, reptiles, and fish, and many species of butterflies, orchids, monkeys, parrots, and pumas. The national park is a nature lover's paradise because of the myriad species of tropical flora found there.

The United Nations Educational, Scientific and Cultural Organization (UNESCO) declared the Iguazú Falls a World Heritage Site in 1986.

The *gauchos*, Argentina's cowboys, ride on horse-back and herd cattle across the *pampas*.

THE PAMPAS

More than two-thirds of Argentina's population live in the *pampas*. The nation's main economic activities are centered in this region. The capital, Buenos Aires, is located here. Most big cities, industries, and important transportation facilities are also located in this part of the country.

The *pampas* are flat and fertile plains with a temperate climate. They stretch over the central part of the country, from the Atlantic Ocean to the Andes Mountains. The *pampas* cover one-fifth of Argentina's land area.

The word *pampas* comes from a Guaraní Indian word meaning "level land." Visitors to Argentina are often astounded when they see the *pampas* stretching to the horizon in all directions, with barely a tree or rock to catch the eye, and looking as flat as the sea. Much of the country's chief crops— wheat, corn, flax, and alfalfa—are grown in the rich soil of the *pampas*. While there is plenty of rain in the eastern *pampas*—about 40 inches (102 cm) a year—the climate is drier on the western plains, where vast herds of cattle graze.

THE ANDES

The western part of Argentina, bordering Chile, is marked by the huge Andes mountain range. Although the earliest Spanish settlements were located in the Andes, only about 15 percent of the population currently lives in this rugged area. A small group of indigenous Indians raise sheep in the northern part of the Argentine Andes. Miners dig for iron ore, uranium, and other metals in this region.

Just east of the Andes lies a region called the Piedmont. Farmers grow export crops such as sugarcane, corn, cotton, and fruit in the low mountains and desert valleys in this region. Most Argentine wines are made from the grapes of San Juan in the vineyards near Mendoza in the Piedmont. The region's dry climate, sandy soil, and year-round sunshine are ideal for the wine industry.

West of Mendoza rises Mt. Aconcagua, the highest peak in the Western Hemisphere. Aconcagua means "stone guard" in an indigenous dialect. The Uspallata Pass, located near Mt. Aconcagua, leads into Chile at a height of 12,600 feet (3,840 m).

Mt. Aconcagua is the highest mountain in both North and South America.

THE SOUTHERNMOST TOWN IN THE WORLD

The southernmost town in the world, Ushuaia ("oo-shoo-AH-yah"), is situated in Argentina. Ushuaia's weather is almost always chilly, and the nearby mountains are usually snowcapped. The 20,000 people who live in Ushuaia can look south, across the waters of the

Beagle Channel, toward the South Pole, some 650 miles (1,046 km) away. People in Ushuaia have only about seven hours of daylight in the winter. In the summer, they enjoy daylight for about 17 hours each day.

PATAGONIA

Patagonia covers more than a quarter of Argentina; the region has dry, windswept plateaus, deep canyons, and stretches of cool desert under the shadow of the Andes. Western Patagonia boasts beautiful resort areas around lakes and mountains; the far south has a cool, foggy, and stormy climate. Patagonia does not experience summer, but ocean currents help to moderate winter temperatures. Only about 1 to 3 percent of Argentina's population lives in Patagonia.

Due to poor soil and little rainfall, most of the land in Patagonia is not suitable for farming. To increase agricultural activity in this region, the government has built irrigation canals.

At the southern tip of South America is the island of Tierra del Fuego, or Land of Fire. In 1520, Ferdinand de Magellan named the island after the Ona and Yagana Indian campfires he saw there. In the 1880s, European settlers and Chileans arrived on the island. They built large ranches for raising sheep and irrigated farmlands to grow vegetables and fruit. One-third of Tierra del Fuego is Argentine territory; the rest of the islands belong to Chile.

ARGENTINA'S WATERS

More than 1,600 miles (2,574 km) of Argentina's length is bounded by the Atlantic Ocean and dotted with large bays. The most important bay is formed by the Río de la Plata, the longest river in Argentina. The Paraná River and its tributaries drain northern and much of central Argentina. The Río de la Plata and the Paraná River are natural boundaries and important arteries in Argentina.

The drainage patterns of Argentina's rivers and lakes are greatly affected by the height of the Andes Mountains. In the south, a number of Argentine lakes empty into the Pacific Ocean through Chile. After heavy rains, however, these lakes pour their extra water into the Atlantic Ocean. This happens because the lakes sit almost directly on top of the continental divide, an imaginary line that directs rivers to flow either east or west.

Visitors to Argentina are often impressed by the country's unique natural beauty. Lake Nahuel Huapí covers 200 square miles (518 square km) at 2,500 feet (762 m) above sea level. This beautiful lake is located in a nature reserve and resort area in the southern Andes. The Perito Moreno Glacier in Patagonia moves 5 yards (4.5 m) a day, shattering icebergs in its path and raising a dramatic explosion of spray.

COLORFUL WILDLIFE

A variety of animals live in Argentina, including the armadillo, opossum, coatimundi, tapir, jaguar, howler monkey, giant anteater, and puma, or mountain lion.

Some unusual species are also found. The guanaco is a small animal related to the camel but without a hump. It is the common ancestor of the llama, alpaca, and vicuña, animals that roam the northern Andean plateau. The vizcacha burrows underground tunnels in the *pampas*. These tunnels often trip horses and cattle. The capybara of the tropical forests is the world's largest rodent. It can weigh more than 110 pounds (50 kg). The Patagonian cavy is similar to the guinea pig.

Visitors to Patagonia are impressed by the picturesque wildlife of the southern coasts; a great number of dolphins, penguins, and sea lions make their home in this region. The Valdés Peninsula, a large nature reserve on the Atlantic coast, supports herds of huge elephant seals as well as groups of large ostrich-like birds called rheas, guanacos, and many other species of birds and animals.

Argentine birds include flamingos, herons, parrots, black-necked swans, and crested screamers. Other birds, such as the tinamou, a relative of the ostrich; the albatross, a large, web-footed seabird; and the Andean condor, a vulture currently in danger of extinction, also live in Argentina.

THE WORLD'S OLDEST DINOSAUR

In 1988, a scientist from the University of Chicago made an amazing discovery. He and his team uncovered the full skeleton of the oldest dinosaur ever recorded. The discoverers named the dinosaur *Herrerasaurus* to honor Victorino Herrera, the goat farmer who led them to the find. It is estimated that *Herrerasaurus* lived 230 million years ago, when most of the earth's land formed a single supercontinent called Pangaea. The meat-eating *Herrerasaurus* was about 6 feet (1.8 m) long and weighed 300 pounds (136 kg). It had sharp teeth like a shark's, talons like an eagle's, and hind legs like those of an ostrich.

HISTORY

ARGENTINA'S indigenous peoples hunted and gathered across the Chaco, the Pampas and Patagonia. They originated in Asia and crossed the Bering Strait that joined Siberia with North America in prehistoric times.

When the first European settlers arrived, approximately 300,000 indigenous Indians lived in Argentina. A combination of war, diseases brought by the Europeans such as smallpox and measles, and intermarriage greatly reduced the indigenous population. Today, less than 3 percent of Argentines are pure Indians.

EXPLORERS ARRIVE

The first European to land in Argentina is reportedly Juan Díaz de Solís, a Portuguese explorer who sailed into the Río de la Plata estuary in 1516. Solís claimed the land for Spain but was killed by indigenous Indians at a later landing venture. In 1520, Portuguese explorer Ferdinand de Magellan stopped at the same river on his historic voyage around the world.

In 1527, Sebastian Cabot, an Italian serving the Spanish crown, founded the first European settlement near present-day Rosario. It was Cabot who named the river Río de la Plata, or River of Silver, after the silver jewelry worn by the local Indians.

The Cabildo in Buenos Aires used to house the Spanish colonial government.

THE COLONIAL PERIOD The history of Argentina is part of the larger story of the conquest and colonization of South America by the Spanish and Portuguese. The conquest of the Inca Empire of Peru in 1532 by Francisco Pizarro opened the way for colonists. Most of the Spaniards who arrived by sea were eventually driven away by the indigenous Indians and the fear of starvation. The Spaniards who finally settled in Argentina came mainly from Peru and Chile by crossing over the Andes. They founded Argentina's oldest cities—Jujuy, Salta, Tucumán, Mendoza, and Córdoba—in the late 1500s. Argentina was part of the Viceroyalty of Peru until 1776, when the Viceroyalty of the Río de la Plata was established. Horses, sheep, and cattle brought from Spain easily multiplied in the fertile new land.

During the 1600s, Spain's economy declined. The Spanish government was forced to sell large plots of land in Argentina. Rich Europeans and *criollos* ("kree-OH-zhos"), or people of Spanish descent born in Latin America, bought the land and established huge estates. To herd their wild cattle, the owners hired *gauchos*, who were usually *mestizos* ("mes-TEE-zohs"), or people of mixed indigenous Indian and Spanish blood.

18

José de San Martín is also known as El Libertador, or "the liberator," for his leadership in the fight for independence from Spain in South America. Monuments dedicated to El Libertador dominate the main squares of cities, towns, and villages throughout Argentina. His portrait hangs in every state school and decorates the country's postage stamps.

INDEPENDENCE

In time, wealthy landowners began to resent the Spanish government's interference in their business affairs. The landowners wanted to control trade and keep the wealth they produced at home rather than send it to Spain in the form of taxes to the Spanish crown.

When France attacked Spain in 1807–08, Argentina's *criollos* took advantage of Spain's military vulnerability to fight for independence. On May 25, 1810, Argentina declared its independence, but King Ferdinand of Spain refused to acknowledge this declaration.

The Argentine national hero, General José de San Martín (1778–1850), urged Argentine leaders to formally declare independence from Spain. They did so in Tucumán on July 9, 1816, and the leaders named their country United Provinces of the River Plate.

San Martín then led an expedition across the Andes into Chile and helped drive out Spanish troops there and in Peru, ending Spanish domination in South America.

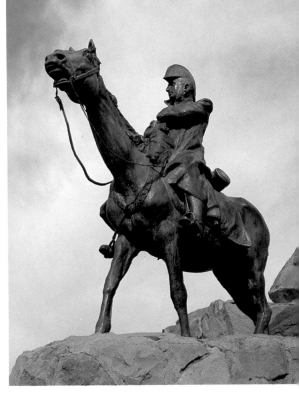

FORGING A NATION

The next 50 years were marked by two major issues: the struggle for power between Buenos Aires and the provinces; and political turmoil under unstable governments. The *porteños* ("por-TAY-nyos"), or residents of the port city of Buenos Aires, quarreled with ranchers in the provinces over control of the country's rural areas. These conflicts almost destroyed trade and the entire Argentine economy.

Dictator Juan Manuel de Rosas ruled Argentina for over 20 years, from 1829 to 1852.

Paris, Impr. lith. de Jacomme et Cie. r de Lancry 12

A constitution drawn up in 1826 gave Buenos Aires control over the interior. The first president of Argentina, Bernardino Rivadavia, was a *porteño*. He was, however, soon overthrown by the rival political party of the rural ranchers, whose leader was in turn killed by members of Rivadavia's party.

The next ruler was a type that would appear frequently in Argentine history—the strongman, or *caudillo* ("cow-DEE-zhoh"). Juan Manuel de Rosas (1793–1877), a landowner from the *pampas*, ruled Argentina from 1829 to 1852. He persecuted and murdered many of his political enemies and wiped out a great number of indigenous Indians. Rosas was finally overthrown by General Justo José de Urquiza. Rosas escaped to England, where he spent the rest of his life in exile.

THE CONSTITUTION OF 1853

A new constitution, proclaimed in 1853, was drawn based on the model of the U.S. constitution. Urquiza then became president of a new confederation of provinces. In 1860, Argentina officially adopted its present name, taken from *argentum*, the Latin word for "silver." The province of Buenos Aires at first refused to join the confederation, becoming a member only after a civil war. Buenos Aires then became the nation's capital. General Bartolomé Mitre took over as president of the 14 united provinces of the Argentine Republic.

During this period, President Domingo Faustino Sarmiento (1811–1888), who ruled Argentina from 1868 to 1874, vigorously promoted public education. The country has one of the highest literacy rates in the world—96 percent.

This illustration from the early 1800s shows European immigrants disembarking at the bay of Buenos Aires.

Pressure to obtain more grazing land resulted in the Indian Wars of the late 1870s and early 1880s. During these battles, indigenous Indians in the *pampas* and in the Patagonia were virtually exterminated. Their lands were taken by officers who had led the war against them.

In 1880, the city of Buenos Aires became a federal district, similar to the District of Columbia in the United States.

THE GOLDEN AGE

In the early 1900s, Argentina attracted many immigrants from around the world. Many of them set up businesses, such as this pharmacy, in Buenos Aires.

Some historians call the years from 1880 to the outbreak of World War I in 1914 "the Golden Age" of Argentina's history. Huge numbers of immigrants and a great deal of foreign investment arrived in the country from Europe. A land of natural resources and frontier wilderness, Argentina seemed destined to become one of the world's richest and most powerful nations by the early 20th century. The railroad system expanded rapidly. Refrigerated ships began to carry beef and hides to Europe in 1877, and exports of farm products grew rapidly. Sheep farming became more prominent. By the 1880s, wool constituted half of Argentina's exports.

During this period, streets were paved, broad avenues and parks were built, and majestic public buildings and private homes sprang up. Argentina became the most urbanized country in Latin America.

In 1929, the Great Depression, triggered by the U. S. stock market crash, had an enormous effect on Argentina's economy. Heavily dependent on the export market, the Argentine economy declined sharply during this time. The government of President Hipólito Irigoyen was not able to solve the economic crisis. Army leaders seized this opportunity to remove the president from office in 1930 and install a military government, followed by a series of military dictatorships.

THE PERÓN ERA

The most famous strongman leader in Argentina's history, Colonel Juan Domingo Perón (1895–1974), rose to power during the military regimes of the 1930s and 1940s. He served as minister of labor in a junta (a group of military leaders), becoming president in 1946. He appealed to the working classes by giving them higher wages, pensions, and other benefits and by strengthening their unions. His supporters formed the Peronist party, which remains influential to this day.

Before Perón, foreign countries had tremendous power over Argentina's economy. The British controlled most of the railroads. The United States controlled the auto business. Even the meat-packing industry was dominated by foreigners. Perón increased government spending, took control of many of the country's industries, and built up manufacturing at the expense of farm production, which he taxed heavily. The resulting drop in farm production caused the national income to fall.

Civil liberties were ignored by Perón. He suspended freedom of the press and freedom of speech, altered the constitution to increase his powers, and permitted a second term of office for himself, not allowed under the 1853 constitution. He remained popular with some Argentines because of his personal charm and appeal to the working masses. During his second term, however, his power and popularity declined. He lost the support of the Catholic Church and alienated the army and navy. Perón fled in 1955 and eventually settled in Spain. He left a legacy of debt and inflation, yet his ideas continue to appeal to many Argentines.

"For people like me, Perón was and still is a prophet, a visionary, a father-figure."

—*Alex Huber*

Juan Domingo Perón.

EVITA PERÓN

Perón's beautiful second wife, Eva Duarte de Perón, a former actress, was a powerful leader in her own right until her early death at the age of 33 from cancer. Known as Evita, she was idolized by the urban working class. Evita gained the right to vote for women in 1947 and founded women's political and social service organizations. Her work brought health and welfare benefits to the poor. The masses expressed their affection for Evita by staging huge rallies where she delivered powerful and dramatic speeches. For many, her magnificent jewels and gowns and her rags-to-riches story symbolized a proud and wealthy Argentina.

Evita was born in the poor village of Los Toldos in 1919. She went to Buenos Aires in her teens and became a popular radio actress. Perón, a widower, was 48 and Evita was 24 when they met. She greatly assisted his rise to power. Perón's popularity dropped significantly after her death. Many Argentines viewed Evita as a saint, but the Catholic Church in Rome resisted all pressure to canonize her. Her epitaph in La Recoleta cemetery reads, "Don't cry for me, Argentina, I remain quite near to you."

DISRUPTION

Military dictators alternated with civilian presidents during the years of Perón's exile. In 1956, Perón's constitution of 1949 was replaced by the original constitution of 1853. Taking an anti-Peronist stance, the military government dissolved Perón's political party. The most noted president of this period, Arturo Frondizi (1958–1962), ironically won the presidency with the support of the Peronist factions of rival political parties. He promised to re-establish the Peronist party in exchange for their support.

After a period of strikes and political unrest, the military allowed a Peronist named Héctor José Cámpora to become president in 1973. Later that year, Perón returned from exile. Cámpora resigned, enabling Perón to be elected president in October 1973. Perón named his third wife, Isabel, vice-president and governed briefly until his death the following year at the age of 79.

After being suppressed for many years by military dictatorships, Perón's party returned to power with the support of the people in 1973.

After Perón's death, Isabel became the first woman president in the history of Argentina. During her presidency, inflation rose to over 400 percent and terrorist acts, mainly by the left-wing guerrilla group, the Montoneros, plagued the country.

THE "DIRTY WAR"

In 1976, military leaders arrested Isabel Perón. They seized the government, dissolved the congress, outlawed all political parties, censored the press, and banned all strikes. The new leaders began what is known as the *guerra sucia* ("GAY-rah SUE-see-ah")*,* or "dirty war," against the terrorists. The military government was able to destroy the power of guerrilla groups, but in their campaign, they condoned violence against thousands of innocent people. The government kidnapped and killed many of its opponents, without revealing their fates. These political victims became known as *los desaparecidos* ("lohs day-sah-pah-ray-SEE-dohs), or "the disappeared."

Mothers of "the disappeared" began to demonstrate every Thursday in the Plaza de Mayo, outside the government palace. These women were later called the "Mothers of the Plaza de Mayo." Later investigations revealed that most of the disappeared had been killed. Hundreds of detention centers had been used to torture and kill people. Mass graves were discovered. A government commission described this period as the "greatest tragedy of our history, and the most savage."

Opposite and below: **The Mothers of the Plaza de Mayo. According to a report published in 1986, almost 9,000 Argentines disappeared during the "dirty war."**

27

The Falkland Islands are remote from the rest of the world and desolate, inhabited by about 2,800 people. The islands' economy relies solely on sheep farming.

THE FALKLANDS WAR AND DEMOCRACY

Argentina's economy worsened during the Falklands War in 1982. Although Britain had occupied the islands since 1833, Argentina had claimed sovereignity of them since the early 1800s. The Islas Malvinas, as the islands are called in Argentina, lie about 300 miles (483 km) off the coast of Argentina. The residents are British subjects.

President Leopoldo Galtieri, an army general, hoped to unite the Argentine people behind his government by occupying the islands and taking them back from the British. Argentine troops fought in the air, at sea, and on the islands, but failed to repel the British army. The war lasted 72 tragic days, taking 2,000 Argentine and British lives.

When Argentina surrendered, it did not give up its claim to the islands. Britain maintains a 2,500-man garrison in the Falklands.

It was not until seven years after the war that Argentina and Great

Britain resumed consular ties, air and sea links, and unrestricted trade.

The military defeat in the war led to a call for free elections. Raúl Alfonsín became president in December 1983, restoring the constitution of 1853. Alfonsín brought to trial the military commanders responsible for the "dirty war." Nine commanders were tried, and five received prison sentences. The military was able to prevent the prosecution of lower-ranking officers who, they said, were only following orders.

Economic woes— inflation, unemployment, and falling wages— damaged Alfonsín's popularity. In May 1989, Peronist Carlos Menem was elected president.

The short Falklands War further crippled Argentina's weak economy and cost the lives of many British and Argentine soldiers.

Riots over high food prices led Alfonsín to resign in June, allowing Menem to take office five months early. Menem altered the constitution in 1994 to allow himself to run for a second term, which he won. In 1999, Fernando de la Rúa won the election; he is the current president.

President de la Rúa has extensive political experience; he was elected Chief of Government of Buenos Aires in 1996. The de la Rúa administration is working hard to attract investors to Argentina in order to improve the country's economic situation, which is currently suffering from a recession.

GOVERNMENT

ARGENTINA'S OFFICIAL NAME is República Argentina, or Argentine Republic. The republic was established on May 1, 1853, the year the constitution was adopted. Like the U.S. constitution, the Argentine constitution calls for an elected president and congress. The president and vice-president must be born in Argentina. They serve a four-year term and can be re-elected once. Every Argentine 18 years old and above can vote.

Power is divided between the executive, legislative, and judicial branches of the government. This creates a system of checks and balances that is meant to prevent one person or branch from gaining complete control of the nation.

The president appoints a cabinet of ministers to head the executive departments of the government. The vice-president leads the senate and becomes president if the president can no longer serve.

The Argentine Congress is made up of two houses, the chamber of deputies and the senate. The chamber of deputies has 257 members elected directly by the people. Deputies serve for four years. The senate comprises 72 members chosen by the provincial legislatures. Three senators represent each of the 23 provinces and the Federal District of Buenos Aires. Senators serve for six years.

In 2001, a new electoral system for the senate will take effect. Under the new plan, all senators will compete for seats, and the winners will draw lots to see whether they will hold office for two, four, or six years. This initiates a cycle in which a third of the senate will be renovated every two years.

Above: **Argentina has two main political parties: The Radical Civic Union, or Radical Party, attracts mainly middle-class voters; the Justicialist Liberation Front, also called the Peronist Party, targets the working class.**

Opposite: **The cabildo, or municipal council, in Buenos Aires was the site of the meeting where the Argentine movement for independence from Spain began on May 25, 1810.**

THE JUDICIARY

The Argentine judiciary, or system of courts and judges, is influenced by the judicial systems of the United States and Western Europe. The president appoints, with approval from the senate, the nine members of the Supreme Court and the judges of the Federal Courts of Appeal. All judges are appointed for life.

Each province has its own system of lower and higher courts. Judges in the provinces are appointed by the local governors. Local governments have limited powers, since the president can remove the governor of a province and call for new provincial elections.

The constitution establishes trial by jury for criminal cases, but this is rarely practiced. The death penalty was re-introduced in 1976—more as a deterrent than as punishment—for the killing of government, military police, and judicial officials and for other terrorist activities. By 1990, the death penalty was abandoned.

The Palace of Justice in Buenos Aires.

THE ARMED FORCES

The president is commander-in-chief of the armed forces. Military conscription, a system which requires young, healthy male—and at times female—citizens to serve in the nation's armed forces for a specific number of years, was abolished in 1995.

At times, the armed forces have been Argentina's strongest political force. Argentine military leaders have overthrown civilian governments on many occasions during the last century. Some of these military coups were bloody, while others were less violent.

The constitution of 1853 guaranteed Argentines freedom of speech and religion and gave them the right of public assembly and private property. These and other supposedly inalienable civil liberties often suffered under military regimes. In addition, the "dirty war" was the only time in the history of the republic when the government actually set aside and ignored the constitution to achieve its goals.

Since military takeovers have often disrupted constitutional governments in Argentina, no Argentine president in the last century has been able to achieve his or her government's goals or remain in office long without the support of the military. The greatest challenge in governing Argentina has been to develop a democratic government stable enough to withstand the pressure and demands of powerful self-interest groups and the military.

FERNANDO DE LA RÚA

President Fernando de la Rúa must make tough choices in order to reduce Argentina's debt and increase its productivity.

Argentina's newest president, Fernando de la Rúa, was born in Córdoba Province in 1937. He studied law at the University of Córdoba, receiving his degree and a gold medal for academic excellence at the age of 21. He then pursued a doctorate degree in law.

De la Rúa was elected to the presidency in 1999 with 48.5 percent of the popular vote. He is a member of the Radical Civic Union party, or UCR. His vice-president, Carlos Alberto Alvarez, is a member of the Front for a Country in Solidarity party, or FREPASO. Together de la Rúa and Alvarez have formed a strong political alliance.

De la Rúa entered politics at the age of 26 as an aide to the Minister of the Interior under President Arturo Illia (1963–1966). De la Rúa was first elected senator in 1973 and served until the military coup disbanded democratic government in 1976. In 1991, he became the head of his party's national committee, and in 1992, he was once again elected senator.

The biggest challenge facing this president is the national deficit and economic recovery, following severe crises under his predecessor, Carlos Saúl Menem. De la Rúa's program includes cutting government spending while increasing taxes. De la Rúa has also negotiated an emergency loan with the International Monetary Fund and is trying to help indebted provincial governments.

THE STATE FLAG AND THE COAT OF ARMS

The sun with a human face, called the "Sun of May," appears on the state flag, which was adopted in 1818, and on the coat of arms. The sun represents Argentina's freedom from Spain. The colors, light blue and white, were worn by Argentine soldiers who fought off British invaders in 1806–07.

The coat of arms shows two hands clasped and surrounded by a laurel wreath. The background colors match the colors of the flag. In the back is a red "liberty cap" on a pole. The sun rises from the top of the wreath.

ECONOMY

THE SPANISH EXPLORERS named Argentina after the silver they expected to find in the new land. In the end, they didn't find mineral resources. So they brought cattle and sheep from Europe and cultivated wheat and other grains. These became Argentina's main economic resources.

Argentina has the potential to become one of the most prosperous countries in Latin America. Food is plentiful and cheap. Poverty, starvation, and malnutrition that plague many countries on the continent were virtually unknown in Argentina, until the present economic crisis.

Half of Argentina's total land area is used for pasture. The soil is rich and productive in the roughly 9 percent of the land that is cultivated for crops. The main farm crops include corn, wheat, soybeans, and sorghum. Grapes, apples, citrus fruits, sugarcane, *yerba mate*, tobacco, cotton, and tea are also grown. From grapes come a variety of fine wines.

Many people are employed in agriculture, which accounts for 7 percent of Argentina's gross domestic product (GDP). The GDP is a measure of the goods and services produced in a country.

Argentina is famous for beef production. The British cattle breeds of Aberdeen Angus, Hereford, and Shorthorn and the French Charolais are particularly popular. Patagonia and other dry parts of Argentina are sheep-breeding regions; sheep's wool is a major export.

Farmers raise large numbers of pigs and poultry. The dairy industry is also quite extensive.

Opposite and below: **Early explorers expected to find huge deposits of silver in Argentina. Instead they found wealth in the rich soil and vast grazing lands.**

Argentina is one of the world's biggest producers and exporters of beef, wool, wine, and wheat.

MANUFACTURING AND SERVICE INDUSTRIES

The manufacturing sector accounts for about 29 percent of Argentina's GDP and employs close to one-fifth of the workforce. Argentina's industrial base is quite diverse, thanks to the bounty of the *pampas*. The chief industry remains the processing of meat and other food products. Other industries include textiles, leather goods, chemicals, metals, printing, lumber, fishing, automobiles, railroad cars, and consumer goods. The factories are highly concentrated in and around Buenos Aires.

The service sector accounts for 64 percent of Argentina's GDP and employs the majority of the workforce. Workers in the service sector include those in the local, state, and federal governments, the military, schools, hospitals, stores, restaurants, and banks. Also of particular importance are workers in the fields of transportation and communications, as their contributions help to build the infrastructure of the economy.

NATURAL RESOURCES

In addition to the rich, fertile soil of the *pampas*, Argentina has abundant natural resources. It has enough natural gas reserves to last at least another 60 years. An extensive pipeline system links the natural gas fields with important industrial centers.

Oil and hydroelectric energy sources are being developed. Petroleum supplies about 70 percent of the energy used in Argentina. The most important oil fields are located in Patagonia and the Piedmont. Argentina is one of the chief oil-producing countries in Latin America. Hydroelectric plants supply about two-fifths of the country's electricity.

Argentina's mineral reserves are still largely untouched. Among the minerals found are beryllium, coal, copper, iron, lead, manganese, tin, tungsten, and zinc.

Although there are large forest reserves, especially in the northeast and the south, the timber industry is still fairly small.

The government as well as private companies are investing in the development of the nation's resources. This has lead to the exploitation of new quarries, mines, and oil wells. The building of new roads, dams, and factories has also created new job opportunities and fostered development in rural areas and economic growth.

Oil derricks are a common sight in Argentina. The country is self-sufficient in crude petroleum and petroleum products.

Argentina is famous for the Quebracho tree. The tree yields hard wood that can be used as building material, and its extract is used for tanning hides.

Cowhide provides leather for making shoes and jackets.

IMPORTS AND EXPORTS

Argentina exports about two-thirds more than it imports. Its chief exports are grain, meat, wool, hides, vegetable oils, fruit, vegetables, nuts, and manufactured goods. Exports to Brazil account for 24 percent of Argentina's total export figures; its exports to the European Union account for 21 percent; and its exports to the United States account for 11 percent.

Argentina's chief imports are industrial chemicals, non-electrical machinery, transportation equipment, iron, steel, and coffee. Its imports from the European Union account for 28 percent of Argentina's total imports; the United States accounts for 22 percent, and Brazil accounts for 21 percent.

To further improve the balance of trade, Argentina strives to increase the production of goods for the export market by manufacturing products locally. It now produces nearly all consumer goods it once imported, such as cars, refrigerators, and television sets. One drawback to this policy is the fact that Argentines may miss out on buying cheaper goods made in countries with low labor costs.

INFLATION AND FOREIGN DEBT

The people of Argentina enjoy one of the highest standards of living in South America, yet the modern Argentine economy pales in comparison to past statistics. In the 1920s, Argentina was the eighth-largest economy in the world; by 1987, its economy ranked 58th worldwide.

In the 1930s, after World War I and the Great Depression, the Argentine government began an economic strategy known as import-substitution. By imposing high tariffs on all imported goods, the government aimed to protect, and thereby develop, local industries. The goal of the governments at the time and during the following 40 years was to make Argentina a self-sufficient country, producing its own agricultural and manufactured goods. By the 1970s, this goal had been achieved. The government's focus on industrial development, however, resulted in poorer agricultural output. In addition, high government spending on the industrial sector as well as heavy borrowing from international funds caused exhorbitant inflation rates in the 1980s, rising as high as 1,000 percent.

During the Perón era, extensive social welfare services, established to help Argentines live more comfortably, were blamed for high government spending and a high inflation rate.

Argentines flock from the rural areas to Buenos Aires, hoping for better job opportunities. Many, however, discover that the country's 15 percent unemployment rate means that jobs are just as difficult to find in the cities as in the countryside.

ARGENTINA IN THE NEW MILLENNIUM

Argentina faces many difficult decisions in its efforts to sustain strong social programs while producing goods that can compete in the modern global economy.

In the last decade, Argentina suffered some severe economic crises. In 1991, the Menem administration tied the local currency, the peso, to the U.S. dollar, meaning that one peso would be worth one U.S. dollar. The government also limited the amount of money circulating by tying it to real reserves held by the national bank. This was done in an effort to stop the country's high inflation rate.

Although the Menem government succeeded in lowering Argentina's inflation rate, the country was severely affected by the economic crisis in Mexico in 1995 and anxiety about the fate of Brazil's economy, the region's largest, in 1998. These events provoked rising interest rates and capital flight from Argentina, as many citizens and private companies lost confidence in the country's economy. As a consequence, they withdrew their savings and deposited them in overseas banks. In 1999, after sustained blows, the

For over 40 years, Argentina manufactured most of the cars and buses it needed to meet local demand. After the liberalization of its market, however, imported cars are also available to the Argentine consumer.

The stock exchange in Buenos Aires, Argentina.

Argentine GDP showed a negative 3 percent growth rate.

De la Rúa, who took office in 1999, inherited an ailing economy with a foreign debt totaling U.S.$149 billion, or 2.5 percent of the annual GDP. De la Rúa has made a deal with the International Monetary Fund for a U.S.$7.4 billion loan to help pay Argentina's debts. In return, de la Rúa is expected to make changes in Argentina's strict labor code, alleviate the financial situation of highly-indebted provinces, improve tax administration, and increase efficiency in public services in order to attract more foreign investment. These are difficult challenges to de la Rúa's administration, but they are necessary if the country is to regain some of the capital it lost in the last decade of the century.

Although about 36 percent of Argentines live below the poverty line, de la Rúa's policies and economic direction are slowly attempting to revive local and international confidence in the Argentine economy.

ENVIRONMENT

A MODERN, INDUSTRIALIZED COUNTRY, Argentina faces a number of environmental challenges. The air in the big cities is polluted by motor vehicle emissions and industrial waste, while soil farming areas is slowly being eroded from intense farming. Many Argentines have pressured the government to agree to and comply with a number of international agreements to protect the natural environment at home and abroad.

NATURAL WEALTH

One of the largest countries in the world, spanning a few climatic zones and ecosystems, Argentina has a wealth of biodiversity and natural beauty. The Argentine climate and landscape vary from subtropical in the north to subantarctic in the south, from rainy coasts and river-fed plains in the east to dry semi-deserts and mountains in the west.

Above: **A family of empire penguins in Patagonia, near the Antarctica.**

Opposite: **Many species of deer make their home in Argentina.**

Across these regions live many different species of plants, including grasslands in the *pampas*, virgin rain forests in the north, flowering cacti in the Chaco semi-desert of the northwest, and thorn forests and monkey-puzzle forests in the south. In addition to its diverse flora, Argentina is also home to some of the continent's most amazing animals. The *pampas* and Patagonia regions are home to several kinds of hoofed animals, including the wild boar, axis deer, fallow deer, red deer, mouflon, wild goat, and black antelope. River-dwelling mammals include the giant Brazilian otter and marine otter. The mountain lion, or puma, makes its home in the mountains, while armadillos inhabit the plains. Coastal waters host a variety of sea creatures, such as whales, seals, and penguins.

Habitat destruction is probably the single greatest threat to Argentina's wildlife. Human settlement and farming have caused serious damage to the natural environment. In the north, cattle ranchers have destroyed grassland areas to make way for pastures. In the south, sheep farming has encroached on natural habitats.

There are 28 endangered animal species in Argentina, and another seven are close to becoming endangered. Of these 35 species, birds make up the majority. Birds suffer the most when forests are cut down to make way for towns. The list of endangered birds reads like a collection of paint colors: purple-barred ground dove, red-spectacled parrot, blue-throated macaw, purple-bellied parrot, ochre-breasted pipet, and saffron-cowled blackbird.

The southern river otter and marine otter are at risk of extinction, as are the giant armadillo and lesser fairy armadillo. Off the coast, the blue, rorqual, and finback whales are also in need of protection.

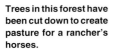

Trees in this forest have been cut down to create pasture for a rancher's horses.

DESERTIFICATION IN THE GRAN CHACO

In Argentina's northwest, near the border with Bolivia and Paraguay, economic pressures are destroying both the natural environment and cultural diversity. This area is part of the Gran Chaco, a semiarid region with low rainfall and few waterways. The Gran Chaco is home to indigenous peoples, who have learned to survive under conditions of intense heat and water scarcity, through gardening, gathering, hunting, and fishing. One of the indigenous groups, the Wichí (*below*), has been active in letting the world know about the destruction of their environment.

Recently, due to pressure from the government to increase the production of beef, ranchers have begun moving their herds deeper into the Gran Chaco. Cattle are not indigenous to the environment, and as they graze, they destroy local plantlife, stripping the land of its natural vegetation and leaving it exposed to the heat of the sun. Fewer plants survive as the ground becomes harder and dryer. This hardening and drying of the ground is called desertification.

The Wichí are petitioning the provincial government in Salta to recognize their claim on the land and to protect the land from further damage. If the area is developed without careful environmental planning, the Wichí may lose their land and their culture.

"Years pass and our lands become impoverished, because the people who have come from the outside to occupy them know not how to manage them. Years pass and we become poorer."

—Quoted in a Wichí appeal for international support

ENVIRONMENTAL PROTECTION EFFORTS

Argentina is a signatory to a number of international accords that aim to protect the world's natural heritage. Argentina recognizes recommendations set out in international protocols on biodiversity, climate change, endangered species, hazardous waste, marine dumping, the nuclear test ban, ozone layer protection, and whaling, for example. In addition, the Argentine government has set aside more than 20 national parks in an effort to protect fragile environments. One of these, Península Valdés in Patagonia, has been designated a World Heritage Site by the United Nations. Península Valdés has been declared a site for the preservation of marine mammals. Southern elephant seals, sea lions, southern right whales, and orcas breed in and around the peninsula.

Argentina has also been active in protecting the earth's ozone layer. The country is a world leader in setting voluntary targets for reducing greenhouse gas emissions such as carbon monoxide.

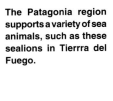

The Patagonia region supports a variety of sea animals, such as these sealions in Tierrra del Fuego.

ANTARCTICA

Argentina, along with Australia, Chile, France, New Zealand, Norway, and the United Kingdom, claim territory in Antarctica. All seven nations, along with 35 others, signed the Antarctic Treaty in 1959. The treaty took effect in 1961 and was strengthened in 1991 by the Protocol on Environmental Protection, which defines Antarctica as a "natural reserve devoted to peace and science."

Only a few scientific reasearch teams are allowed at any one time to live in Antarctica, the world's largest protected nature reserve. Of the countries that send out research teams to Antarctica, Argentina maintains the greatest number of science stations, with six year-round stations and seven summer stations.

Understanding Antarctica is critical to understanding global climate changes, since it is over this continent that scientists have discovered the thinning of the atmospheric layer called the ozone.

"It is in the interest of all mankind that Antarctica shall continue to be used forever for peaceful purposes and shall not become the scene or object of international discord."

—Antarctic Treaty, 1961

AMAZING FACTS ABOUT ANTARCTICA

- It is the highest continent in the world, with an average elevation of 7,550 feet (2,300 m).
- It is the size of the United States and Mexico combined, with 5.4 million square miles (14 million square km) of territory.
- The diameter of the continent is 3,450 miles (5,551 km), or about the distance between Los Angeles and New York.
- The coastline is 19,800 miles (31,858 km) long, or about the distance from Anchorage, Alaska to the southernmost tip of Chile.
- There is no vegetation whatsoever; 98 percent of the continent is ice throughout the year, while 2 percent is barren rock.
- The ice packs and frigid waters are home to the emperor penguin, the largest of penguins, weighing up to 65 pounds (30 kg) and standing over 3 feet (90 cm) tall.

HOPE FOR TOMORROW

Protecting the environment is not limited to passing laws or even setting aside nature reserves, but these are essential first steps. Argentina has led the way among South American countries in taking these first steps and in trying to protect its natural heritage. Argentina is also a world leader in setting voluntary greenhouse gas emission targets. The country's greatest challenge today, however, lies in finding a balance between meeting its needs for economic growth and preserving its natural environment.

Sunflowers bloom in the fertile fields of La Pampa Province. Introducing crops that are suitable to the natural soil of each region is one way of increasing economic productivity without severely damaging the natural environment.

ARGENTINES

THE HEART OF ARGENTINA is its people. Argentina has a population of almost 37 million people.

The typical Argentine does not look particularly "South American." The high cheekbones, darker skin tones, and coal black hair of the indigenous Indians and the *mestizos* and *mulatos* are not characteristic of the crowds on Argentina's streets. Most Argentines look European.

Most Latin American countries have large populations of *mestizos* and people of African descent. In contrast, about 85 percent of Argentines are of European—mostly Italian and Spanish—descent. The remaining 15 percent are *mestizo*, Indian, and other groups.

As large numbers of Europeans migrated to Argentina, they tended to form their own neighborhoods. Buenos Aires and other large cities still have ethnic neighborhoods where the special foods and traditions of different European countries are preserved. Some of these groups publish newspapers in their own languages. They also run schools, hospitals, and clubs mainly targeted at members of their ethnic group but often open to all other members of society.

Argentina's largest ethnic group is the Italian community. About four out of ten people in Argentina are of Italian descent, while about three out of ten trace their heritage back to Spain. Most of the Italian immigrants settled in and around Buenos Aires.

OTHER ETHNIC ROOTS

Argentina once had the largest British community outside Great Britain. British expatriates were influential in developing Argentina's railway, telephone, electricity, gas, and steamship services. They brought sports such as soccer, rugby, cricket, polo, and tennis. They even imported cattle from England. Their descendants are called Anglo-Argentines. The Falklands War between Argentina and Great Britain presented them with a potential conflict of loyalties, but most sided with Argentina.

In addition, more than one million Europeans came to Argentina following World War II. Europe's loss was Argentina's gain. Along with the numerous Italian, Spanish, English, and Welsh immigrants, Argentina was also enriched by people of Austrian, Dutch, French, German, Irish, Jewish, Polish, Portuguese, Russian, Swiss, Chinese, Japanese, and Syrian descent. Immigrants have also come from neighboring South American countries, largely for political or economic reasons. More recently, newcomers have arrived from Korea and Southeast Asia.

Argentina's population consists mostly of people from different European countries, such as Italy, Spain, France, Britain, Russia, Germany, and Poland.

SOCIAL CLASSES

From the mid-18th to mid-19th century, political and social life in Argentina was shaped by the landed aristocracy—the big rural landowners. Many had close ties to Britain and its culture. Members of the upper class considered themselves among the world's most sophisticated people.

When the major waves of European immigrants arrived in Argentina in the late 1800s, they found that the rural areas were controlled by the landed aristocracy. The newcomers could not easily own land or houses in the countryside, so they settled in the cities, especially in Buenos Aires.

Argentina's large and prosperous cities enabled immigrants to find jobs and education and become part of the middle class. The urban middle class today includes workers in small businesses as well as government officials and professionals.

In the past, the landed aristocracy held most of the political power. Today, leaders in industry and commerce, military officers, and professionals exercise considerable power in determining how the country is run. As is the case in many other countries, social classes in Argentina are still largely based on money, education, and family background.

Among the wealthy are ranchers, or *estancieros* ("es-tahn-see-EH-ros"), who own large estates and herds of cattle in the country, but who reside in the cities. They work their farms and ranches with their families and with the help of hired hands.

Since the 1930s, large numbers of people have left the countryside to seek work in the larger cities. Many found only part-time work and have become part of a poor lower class living in slum conditions.

THE PROUD GAUCHOS

The *gauchos* of the past were a special group of Argentine men—mostly *mestizos*—who roamed the *pampas* on horseback. They have become folk heroes, inspiring Argentines even today, as symbols of strength and individualism. A much smaller number of *gauchos* still work on cattle ranches in Argentina.

Like the cowboys of the North American West, the legendary *gauchos* were excellent horsemen. They tamed wild horses, herded cattle, and exhibited skill and courage in everything they did. They could find their way on the plains under any circumstances. By chewing grass, they could tell whether there was water nearby and whether it was salt or fresh. They could tell directions from the lay of the grass and count the number of riders by the sound of the horses' hooves.

The *gauchos* often led rugged lives with few comforts. They lived in small homes with mud walls and floors, a straw roof, and no windows. The *gauchos* were proud, self-reliant, and tough. They fought for survival against the forces of nature and against invaders. During colonial times, they opposed the authority of Spain. Later, they lived in opposition to the new settlers who fenced in the open range.

During the 19th century, the *gauchos'* main job was to transport cattle to the markets in Buenos Aires. The building of roads and railroads and the fencing in of the *estancias* changed the traditional role of the *gauchos*. Although fewer in number, they still work on the *pampas*, driving tractors, repairing engines, and vaccinating cattle.

Argentine *gauchos* are known around the world for their thick leather belts, decorated with silver pieces and sometimes old silver coins.

The traditional *gauchos* adopted the use of bolas from the indigenous Indians. A bola is a long rope with two or three ends tied to hard balls covered with leather. Bolas were used for fighting and hunting, especially the pursuit of the rhea, a bird similar to the ostrich. When thrown at a running target, the bola wraps itself around the legs, tripping the animal and tying its legs. *Gauchos* still exhibit their legendary horsemanship skills at rodeos.

The *gauchos* of the past survived on a diet of meat and *yerba mate*, a holly tea. A typical picture of a *gaucho* shows him on horseback or at rest, singing and strumming a guitar or sipping *yerba mate* from a hollowed-out gourd through a metal straw.

THE CRIOLLOS

In colonial times, *criollos* ("kree-OH-yohs") were people born to Spanish parents in Argentina. Later, the word was used to describe the descendants of the early Spanish settlers, as opposed to the descendants of later waves of European immigrants. Today, the term *criollo* is also used to describe a person who lives in the country or in a small town.

INDIGENOUS ARGENTINES

The small minority of pure indigenous Argentines live mostly in the isolated areas of the Andes Mountains, the Gran Chaco, Patagonia, and Tierra del Fuego. The Diaguita Indians, for example, live west of Salta at an altitude of 9,800 feet (2,987 m). This area was part of the Incan empire before the Spaniards arrived in South America in the 16th century.

Although the soil is poor, the indigenous Indians farm the mountainsides, growing beans, corn, and potatoes. They use irrigation channels built centuries ago by their Inca ancestors to help in their farming.

Because the air is too thin at this altitude for cattle and

sheep to live, the indigenous Indians use llamas for meat, wool, and transportation. From llama wool, the women weave clothing for their families. They also use the wool to make socks, sweaters, scarves, and blankets, which they sell to tourists.

Each indigenous community has its own distinctive style of dress. Women's hairstyles also differ depending on the region. Most Argentine Indians follow a mix of indigenous and European traditions. Although they may profess to be Christians, many still pray to the gods of the sun, moon, earth, thunder, rain, and lightning.

Opposite top: **An indigenous Argentine holds his catch—a** *gila* **monster. Indigenous Argentines have been forced to relocate to mostly barren lands by powerful landowners.**

Opposite bottom: **An indigenous Argentine girl.**

DISAPPEARANCE OF AFRO-ARGENTINES

Argentina had a significant African population in its early years as a republic. Afro-Argentines were the descendants of slaves imported from Africa by the Spanish in the 16th century. Around 1778, Afro-Argentines constituted about 30 percent of Buenos Aires' population.

The slave trade was outlawed in 1813, and most slaves were freed by 1827. A few, however, did not attain freedom until 1861. After Argentina's independence, most Afro-Argentines continued to suffer discrimination in Argentine society.

Between 1836 and 1887, the percentage of Afro-Argentines in Buenos Aires dropped from 26 percent to 1.8 percent. Historical paintings, prints, and photographs as well as the epic poem *Martín Fierro* depict Afro-Argentines. Descendants of Afro-Argentines are rarely seen today. Their disappearance from Argentina's society remains a mystery.

Some scholars believe that the majority of Afro-Argentines died during the yellow fever epidemic of 1871 or in warfare or disappeared through intermarriages with European colonists.

LIFESTYLE

ARGENTINE SOCIETY is dynamic and evolving, a colorful blend of indigenous and imported cultures. Many Argentines follow customs and traditions brought by their ancestors from their country of origin. Also, Argentina's great geographical diversity has shaped different lifestyles in different regions. The Welsh sheep-ranchers of Patagonia, the indigenous Indian farmers of the Andes, and the city dwellers of Buenos Aires lead entirely different lives.

Yet certain customs and traits are shared by most Argentines: they are strongly nationalistic; they are passionate about the arts; and they love to talk about sports, especially soccer, and politics.

"The Argentines are still trying to figure out if they're European or Latin American, and they are famous throughout Latin America for not having made up their minds yet."

—*Deirdre Ball*

Opposite: **Café culture similar to that in southern Europe forms a big part of Argentine life.**

Left: **A little girl feeds pigeons in a park in Argentina.**

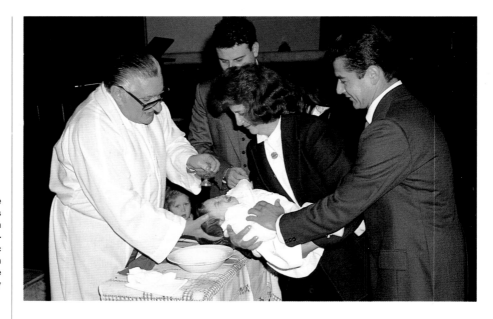

Right and below: **Since many of Argentina's immigrants come from European Catholic countries, Roman Catholic rituals such as baptism and the last rites are observed by many Argentines.**

FROM BIRTH TO DEATH

The majority of Argentines are Roman Catholics, and they follow the traditional practices of the Church to mark important events in their lives. Argentines also follow traditions common to Latin American countries. Children are usually baptized as infants, and they celebrate First Communion

at the age of 8. Girls follow the Latin American tradition of celebrating their fifteenth birthday with a big dance party. This event marks a girl's induction into society.

When a couple gets engaged, they first exchange rings. The woman wears her ring on the fourth finger of her right hand until the wedding, when she shifts it to her left hand. In the wedding ceremony, the groom walks in with his mother and the bride with her father. This custom symbolizes that both are leaving their families and joining as man and wife at the altar.

When people die, their bodies may be either buried or cremated. It is unusual for the body of a dead person to be embalmed and viewed in an open coffin, as was done for Evita Perón.

62

FAMILY LIFE

Family life is very important to Argentines. Family members tend to be nurturing and supportive of one another, and Argentines love to hear compliments about their home and children. A close bond among family members makes them fiercely loyal to one another.

Children are rarely sent away to boarding school; they are quite likely to live at home until marriage and then settle near their parents. University students generally attend classes in their hometown and continue to live with their parents. Workers often come home for lunch.

Argentines care for their elderly parents and frequently invite a widowed parent to live with them. It is not common for the elderly to live in nursing homes.

The extended family of aunts, uncles, and cousins gathers often. This family network is valuable, as gaining entrance into good schools and getting a job are often made possible by family connections.

The father is often a strong, authoritarian figure in the family. Traditionally, he also bears the responsibility of earning enough money to support the family, although women also work and contribute to the family's income.

Young people live by the rules of their families and are influenced by family members through their adolescence and often until after marriage.

Argentines have a strong sense of family. Special occasions such as birthday parties are always celebrated by inviting cousins and other relatives to the home.

CITY LIFESTYLE

The history of Argentina is marked by a long conflict between the city and the countryside. To this day, urban and rural Argentines have contrasting lifestyles.

City life in Argentina reflects the strong influence of the European immigrants. The city plan—the layout of streets, parks, and squares—and architecture of Buenos Aires have a European look. As in Spanish cities, the cathedral and chief government buildings are found facing the plaza, or main square. Argentina's artistic culture, education, fashion, business etiquette, and rules of behavior are also distinctly European.

The Buenos Aires *porteños* are the elite of Argentina. They dominate the government and cultural life of the country. *Porteños* tend to view themselves as sophisticated and well-informed in world affairs. They set trends in behavior and fashion that spread to the provinces. Many *porteños* have little interest in visiting other parts of Argentina. They are sometimes accused of having a superior attitude toward Argentines living outside of Buenos Aires and of viewing non-*porteños*—even those living in cities—as *campesinos* ("kahm-pay-SEE-nohs"), or country folk.

FRIENDSHIP THRIVES IN THE CAFÉ

Argentines love to discuss sports, politics, philosophy, and the arts. In Buenos Aires, particularly, having discussions means lingering in a café talking with friends. There are hundreds of old cafés lining the busy streets of Buenos Aires. The most important feature of a café is its relaxed atmosphere; the meals served are considered much less important. The waiters are trained never to rush customers. The English custom of having tea and snacks in the afternoon lives on in Argentina.

Founded in 1858, the Tortoni is the oldest café in Buenos Aires. It has a charming old billiard room, and the walls are decorated with souvenirs from the many painters and writers who have gathered there over the years. Conspirators and army chiefs have also gone to sip coffee or play a game of chess. Jazz performances add to the atmosphere on weekends.

Because Argentines are often creatures of habit, many prefer to meet over and over again at the same café. The favorite discussion is what it means to be Argentine.

Cafés, restaurants, and clubs stay open very late. The typical workday runs from 9 A.M. to 7 P.M., though sometimes it may extend as late as 10 P.M. It is not uncommon for Argentines to have dinner as late as 10 P.M. or even midnight. Famous for its nightlife, some streets of Buenos Aires are bustling with people long after the clock strikes midnight.

Opposite top: **A country house by the sea.**

Opposite bottom: **In the mountainous Andes region, horses are a common means of transportation.**

THE SUGAR, SALT, AND SPICE OF RELATIONSHIPS

The warmth Argentines show to their family members is often extended to friends. Argentines tend to make physical contact when greeting. They hug and kiss on meeting and leaving one another. When introduced, men shake hands, but close male friends may hug one another. Women friends shake hands and kiss each other on one cheek.

Flirting has a certain style in Argentina. A man may pass a woman on the street and compliment her on her beauty without expecting her to stop or reply. His compliment, called a *piropo* ("pee-ROH-poh"), may be indirect, such as: "It must be lonely in heaven since one of the more beautiful angels descended to earth!" Less poetically, when passing a mature woman, a man might say: "Old but still good."

Women also flirt, making witty remarks and even put-downs that are meant to be heard and enjoyed by their friends. In the words of a common Argentine saying, "in the United States, women are called sweet; in Spain, they are called salty; but in Argentina, women are spicy."

COUNTRY LIFESTYLE

In the countryside, the European influence on lifestyles is less noticeable. Rural Argentines lead different lifestyles according to their economic status. Rich country people live and work on huge ranches, often built as luxurious country estates. Others live on small farms. The poorest people live in homes made of straw and mud with dirt floors.

Rural Argentines tend to see themselves as being more humble, having more common sense, and being in better touch with the land than people in the cities. They sometimes resent what appears to them to be the arrogance of the *porteños*.

The great rivalry between Argentines of the countryside and the people of Buenos Aires, once very heated, no longer erupts into violence. The two different ways of life are today increasingly seen as complementary to one another.

Top and bottom: **Argentina's social divide shows in the contrast between a shanty town and the home of a well-to-do family.**

RICH AND POOR

Economic problems in past decades have widened the social gap between the rich and the poor in Argentina, creating vast differences in lifestyle between the wealthy of Buenos Aires' northern suburbs and the poor of the slums known as *villas miserias* ("VEE-jahs mee-SEH-ree-ahs"). Sometimes the two live only a bus stop away from each other.

In recent years, church and volunteer organizations have joined efforts to raise money to build adequate housing for the shanty town residents of Tigre, a fading resort northwest of the city.

One stumbling block for these organizations is the unwillingness of Argentines to give money to charity, as there have been cases in the past of mismanagement of funds by charitable organizations.

POLITICAL TALK

Under the democratic governments, the Argentine people have gained the right to voice their political views without fear.

In 1945, thousands of workers answered Evita Perón's call to protest her husband's detention by marching in the Plaza de Mayo. Historians mark this event as the day the working class gained real political power.

Street rallies, marches, and people carrying placards on the streets are the traditional ways in which Argentines express their political opinions. Traffic halts for union demonstrators and students singing songs of protest. Political graffiti can be found on many buildings and walls.

During elections, Argentines turn out in large numbers to vote at the polls. Most speak freely about which political party they support and whom they voted for in the last elections.

A street rally in Buenos Aires.

WOMEN

Traditionally, Argentine women did not play a large role in public life. Evita Perón was the first woman to advocate and promote women's rights in Argentina. She is still admired by many feminists for her active role in politics. Evita worked to gain women working benefits and the right to vote.

Argentine men and women have equal rights under the constitution. Since the 1940s, women have become more active in professional jobs. Evita Perón was extremely influential in her husband's administration, and

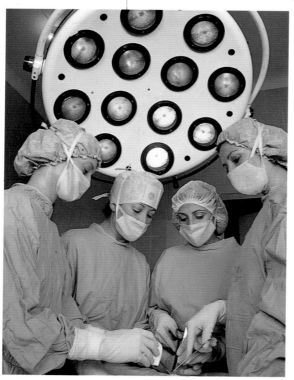

Women, such as these surgeons, excel in almost every professional field in Argentina.

Perón's third wife, Isabel, became president of the country. Also, an increasing number of women work as doctors, lawyers, and architects, among other professions. Through Evita's efforts, divorce was legalized, but this act was reversed shortly after her husband's fall in 1955. Not until 1987 was divorce legalized again.

Women became forceful in public life during the "dirty war" when the courageous "Mothers of the Plaza de Mayo" marched past the Casa Rosada every Thursday, carrying placards inscribed with the names of their missing loved ones. At great personal risk, they demonstrated to end human rights abuses and hold the government accountable for the "disappeared."

Today, large numbers of women are working in business and government, closing the professional gap between men and women that was prevalent in Argentina until recent years.

Selling jewelry at a street stall.

When a woman marries, she keeps her maiden name. If María García marries Juan Adler, she becomes María García de Adler, or Señora García de Adler. Children take the father's last name. Unlike in English, letters are not addressed to "Mr. and Mrs. Juan Adler" but to "Mr. Juan Adler and Mrs.," which reads in Spanish, *"Señor Juan Adler y Señora."*

In the past, women commonly went out accompanied by a man. This custom has changed in recent years, as active participation in business and government has given Argentine women financial and social independence.

In Argentina, abuse of women is usually not brought out in the open. Crimes of rape and incest are considered shameful and frequently are not reported to doctors or the police. Although Argentina is predominantly a Catholic society, the practice of contraception and abortion is common, and there are fewer illegitimate children than in other Catholic countries.

Traditionally, in Argentine restaurants, only men wait on tables. Waitresses are a rare sight.

Seeing a psychiatrist is very common in Argentina. Therapy sessions help people to improve their emotional and mental health.

ARGENTINE ATTITUDES

While some Argentines like to make dramatic gestures, the general tendency is to avoid loud and unusual behavior in public. Nevertheless, Argentines do express their emotions openly, as is typical of most Latin Americans.

A leisurely schedule governs the gathering of friends. People invited to dinner arrive 30 to 60 minutes after the specified time. When invited to a birthday party, guests bring gifts, which are usually opened in their presence.

Many Argentines go to psychiatrists or psychoanalysts, and many of the analysts in Spain are Argentines. Some think psychiatry is popular among Argentines because

people see themselves more as individuals than as part of a group. Argentines tend to be quite concerned with their personal thoughts and feelings.

When you ask for directions on the street, an Argentine may give a detailed, possibly wrong, answer rather than admit that he or she does not know the way to your destination. Keeping up appearances is very important to some Argentines.

Some dramatize their lives or cover up their poverty with a bit of exaggeration. For example, a woman may tell her friends that she was chauffered to the restaurant where they are having lunch when she actually came on the bus. A man may tell a new acquaintance that he lives in a building known for its expensive apartments when he actually lives in a more modest home.

Some Argentines believe in higher powers. A tango dancer, for example, may make the sign of the cross and pray for a successful performance. Some stage performers are known to wear amulets or a "lucky tie" whenever they go on stage.

Argentines are very open about their feelings and are not ashamed of displaying affection in public.

In Argentina, telephone wires are not buried underground. In the financial district of Buenos Aires, thousands of telephone wires are strung together from poles, weaving a complex network that resembles a cobweb.

Nightlife in Buenos Aires. Many shops and restaurants in the cities are open until the early hours of the morning.

SOCIAL AND BUSINESS CUSTOMS

Argentines prefer to do business in person rather than over the telephone. Appointments for business meetings are preferred to unexpected visits to an office.

It is polite to make small talk at the end of a business meeting, rather than leave abruptly when things are settled. Most Argentines prefer not to discuss business during meals. The pace of negotiations is much slower than in the United States and is based more on personal contact.

On a social basis, many people drop in on friends from around 4 to 6 P.M. without calling ahead.

NOSTALGIA IN ARGENTINA

Argentines are said to have a sentimental streak. They remember the past in songs and stories and in the glorification of the *gaucho* as a folk hero. The architecture of the cities is full of reminders of the past—old fountains, wrought-iron gates. Families remember their immigrant past through collections of treasured photographs. Tango music expresses this nostalgia with lyrics that speak of lost loves and unfulfilled dreams.

Social plans are likely to be spontaneous, rather than scheduled weeks in advance.

In Buenos Aires, in particular, people stay out late many nights of the week and seem to survive on little sleep. Shops are closed on Saturday afternoon so that people may rest to prepare themselves for Saturday night activities. On Sundays, families gather for large noon meals. Shops are closed on Sunday.

RELIGION

ROMAN CATHOLICISM is Argentina's official religion. The vast majority of Argentines—about 92 percent—are nominal Catholics. However, less than 20 percent of Argentine Catholics attend church regularly. In general, Argentines take a relaxed view toward religion. However, when the pope visited in 1982 and again in 1987, millions showed their support by flocking to see the spiritual leader.

According to the constitution of 1853, the president and vice-president of Argentina must be Roman Catholic. Also, the government provides some financial support to the Church. The constitution guarantees freedom of religion for all. It also requires that strong relations exist between Church and State, but in an environment of religious pluralism and freedom.

Religious groups can run their own churches, hospitals, social centers, and cemeteries. Religious schools are allowed, but religion is not always taught in public schools. Religious sects can be banned by the government if they appear to threaten public order and morality.

By law, all Argentine children must be registered at birth with names found in a registry of acceptable first names. These are often, but not always, the Spanish names of Catholic saints.

Within the Catholic Church, different groups, or orders, focus on a specific type of social work. Some run hospitals and orphanages; others run schools. Some are missionaries in remote areas of the country; others do work with prisoners and juvenile delinquents.

Opposite: **San Francisco church in Salta Province. Many of Argentina's oldest churches are located in the northern provinces.**

Below: **The opulence of Argentina's colonial churches bears testimony to the past wealth and power of the Catholic Church in the country.**

An Armenian wedding in Argentina. Racial and religious tolerance is characteristic of Argentines.

OTHER RELIGIOUS GROUPS

About 2 percent of Argentines are Protestants. Besides Roman Catholics and Protestants, there are other Christians who belong to the Armenian, Orthodox, and Ukrainian churches. Many Jews came from Europe in the late 19th and early 20th centuries; Jews now make up about 2 percent of the Argentine population and live mostly in Buenos Aires. Muslims, members of other religious groups, and atheists make up the remaining 4 percent of the population.

Writers have called the reverence paid to Evita Perón a kind of religious fervor. After her death, President Juan Perón was unsuccessful in his attempt to have his wife declared a saint by the Catholic Church. Nevertheless, her admirers continue to place fresh flowers at her tomb every day. Believers ask her to grant them favors and to protect them from harm.

In rural areas, *mestizos* have mixed elements of animistic religions with Catholic practices. They pray to the spirits of nature as well as to the Christian god. They hold festivals throughout the year filled with singing and dancing dedicated

A vodoo ritual.

to indigenous gods. Superstition blends with Christianity, as when a person makes the sign of the cross to ward off the "evil eye." Rural shrines to unofficial saints are popular pilgrimage sites in the countryside.

About six weeks before Easter, before the fasting period of Lent, the yearly celebration of Carnival begins. In parts of Argentina, the decorations for Carnival are inspired as much by folk religion as by Christianity.

Magical, occult, and New Age spiritualism have found expression in Argentina too.

The statue of Christ of the Andes, located on the border between Argentina and Chile, was erected to symbolize lasting peace between the two countries.

YAMANA BELIEFS

The Yamana Indians, now extinct, were an ancient aboriginal people who lived at the southern tip of Argentina. Their stories were passed down orally, without ever being put in writing until a priest, Father Martin Gusinde, documented their legends from interviews with the last Yamana survivors in the 1920s.

One Yamana myth tells of a great flood. When the people offended Lexuwakipa, a spirit disguised as an ibis, she sent down so much snow that a huge mass of ice covered the Earth. This took place at a time when men and women were battling each other. Eventually, the men won by seizing the women's secret meeting place, the source of their power.

When the snow began to melt, it flooded all the Earth. The water rose steadily and rapidly. The people struggled to save themselves. Finally, only five mountain peaks remained above water. The water remained level for two full days, then subsided. Practically all the Yamana had drowned; only a few families managed to save themselves. Once the great flood had subsided, the survivors began to rebuild their homes. But ever since, men have ruled over women.

A statue of the Virgin of Luján.

MIRACULOUS STATUES

Incredible tales about miraculous statues abound throughout Argentina. Here are the two of the most famous stories:

THE VIRGIN OF LUJÁN In 1630, before the town of Luján was founded, a man tried to drive an oxcart carrying a statue of the Virgin Mary over a plot of land. But no matter how many oxen were hitched to the cart, the statue would not move. The people decided that the Virgin Mary did not want her statue to leave its original spot, so they unloaded the statue and built a small chapel on the site. Later, a large, richly decorated church was built to house the thousands of pilgrims who began coming to Luján every year to pray to the Virgin Mary. Luján is located about 44 miles (71 km) west of Buenos Aires.

THE CRUCIFIX OF SALTA In the 17th century, a ship carrying a statue of the crucified Christ sank at sea on its way from Spain to the cathedral in Salta Province in Argentina. Miraculously, the statue floated to the coast of Peru, from where it was carried by a horse across the Andes to Salta, a distance of 1,600 miles (2,574 km).

There was a great celebration when the statue arrived safely. After the festivities, the statue was packed and stored away in the cathedral's cellar.

A hundred years later, a major earthquake shook Salta. When the people went to the cathedral to pray, they heard a voice saying that the quakes would not stop until the statue was put in its proper place in the cathedral. The statue was paraded around the city in a procession before being returned to the cathedral, and the quake stopped. Since then, the crucifix of Salta has been paraded around the city every year to commemorate the event.

LANGUAGE

JUST ABOUT EVERYBODY in Argentina speaks Spanish, the country's official language. Spanish is taught in all schools and is the only language used by the Argentine government.

Spanish spoken in Argentina has local variations. The main Spanish dialect in Argentina is slightly different from the Spanish spoken in Spain, but people from both countries usually have no trouble understanding one another.

The influx of immigrants from Italy has influenced Argentine Spanish greatly, giving it an Italian accent and adding to it some Italian words. The influence of Italian is most noticeable around Buenos Aires and in the *pampas*, where many Italians settled. *Buongiorno*, Italian for "good morning," often replaces the Spanish *buenos días* ("boo-EH-nohs DEE-ahs"), and "goodbye" becomes *chau* ("chow"), a variation of the Italian *ciao*.

The *mestizos* in the north use dialects influenced by indigenous Indian languages, though generally these languages have less of an influence in Argentina than in many other South American countries due to the small number of indigenous Indians in Argentina. The descendants of immigrants from Mexico, Bolivia, Chile, and Paraguay who have speak in their own distinctive Spanish dialects.

Above: **Argentines love to chat over a drink.**

Opposite: **Spanish is Argentina's official language. All Argentine school children learn their lessons in Spanish.**

European immigrants and indigenous peoples have lent great variety to Spanish dialects used in Argentina.

OTHER VOICES

English is spoken throughout Argentina as a second language. Other languages, such as German, are still spoken by the descendants of immigrants in the larger towns and cities. Welsh is spoken by the descendants of Welsh immigrants in Patagonia.

Only a small number of the indigenous people of Argentina still speak Guaraní, Quechua, or other Indian languages. The names of these disappearing languages are quite musical: Aymará, Chiriguano, Chorotí, Mataco, Mocoví, Toba, Lule, Ranquel, Moleche, Tehuelche, and Ona. Scholars are making efforts to preserve and record the legends and oral traditions of Argentine Indians before their languages become extinct.

OF GANGSTERS AND TANGO SINGERS

Lunfardo ("loon-FAR-doh") is slang which is related to tango music, popular songs, and the theater. This dialect has influenced Spanish spoken in Buenos Aires since around 1900. *Lunfardo* uses words borrowed from Italian, Portuguese, and many other languages.

Lunfardo began as a form of criminal slang. Words were borrowed, invented, and used in a way that could only be understood by those who used the dialects. *Lunfardo* playfully changes the names of things. For instance, to speak of a person's head, the *lunfardo* speaker might choose words that mean "a bed of fleas," "thinker," "ball," or "the top of a building."

Soon poets and journalists discovered the colorful expressions of *lunfardo* and began to use them in their writing. Tango singers also began to use them in their songs. From 1916, poets wrote works in *lunfardo* with titles such as *Versos Rantifusos* (Street Verses) and *La Crencha Engrasada* (Slicked-Down Hair). The first tango to be sung had *lunfardo* lyrics and was called *Mi Noche Triste* (My Night of Grief). It was sung in 1917 by Carlos Gardel, the most famous of all tango singers.

For a period of time, beginning in the 1940s, the government banned *lunfardo*. Nevertheless, the dialect continued enriching the spoken and written language of Buenos Aires. Over the years, new words were added and old ones dropped. In 1962, a group of scholars, artists, and radio people founded the Lunfardo Academy of Buenos Aires to preserve this distinctive language.

A tango singer expresses himself using *lunfardo* lyrics.

DID YOU KNOW...?

Argentines tend to speak quickly, and they pronounce some consonants differently from the way Spaniards in Europe do. Some "s" sounds in Argentina are pronounced "th" in Spain. To a person used to the sounds of English, Castilian Spanish spoken in Spain sounds almost as if the speaker is lisping. In Argentina, the "ll" sound is pronounced like a soft "j" or "sh." In other Spanish-speaking South American countries, such as Chile, "ll" sounds like a "y."

In written Spanish, question marks and exclamation marks appear not only at the end of a sentence, but also upside down at the beginning of a sentence.

In Spanish, the meaning of a word can change depending on which syllable is stressed. *Papá*, with the stress on the last syllable, means father. *Papa,* with no stress on the final syllable, means potato.

There is no A.M. or P.M. in Argentine Spanish. To say 8 A.M., a speaker must use words that translate as "eight in the morning." Airports and train and bus stations usually use a 24-hour clock. For example, when it is 3 P.M., these clocks read 15:00.

ARGENTINES LOVE TO READ

Argentina has a high literacy rate, and Argentines can read newspapers in Spanish and foreign languages. At least 230 newspapers are published, about 70 in Buenos Aires alone. *La Prensa,* known for its excellent coverage of international news, and *La Nación* are two important dailies, each over 120 years old.

Tourists who have traveled to other Spanish-speaking countries may be confused by the Spanish spoken in Buenos Aires, as *porteños* speak with a heavy Italian accent.

Newspapers published in Buenos Aires are sold throughout most of the country. Major provincial cities also publish their own newspapers. The oldest in print is probably *La Capital,* founded in Rosario in 1867.

The degree of freedom enjoyed by the press has varied under different political regimes. *La Prensa* was seized by Juan Perón's officials in 1949 and was not returned to its owners until 1955. Publications have been banned because they were considered immoral or pro-communist by the government. In 1976, a period of book censorship began, and scholars were persecuted for their ideas. The present government allows artists and the media the freedom to express their views and criticisms.

The *Buenos Aires Herald,* founded in 1876, is the most prestigious English-language newspaper in South America. It is sold in all major cities in Argentina.

Streetside stalls sell magazines and newspapers in Argentine cities.

More than 4,000 publications come out every year in Argentina. The country's first magazine, *La Ilustración Argentina,* was printed in 1853. Picture magazines, such as *Gente* and *Siete Días,* are very popular. Among the best-known literary magazines are *Ficción, Sur,* and *Nosotros.* Readers like to browse in the country's 8,000 bookstores, many of which are open 24 hours a day.

RADIO AND TELEVISION

Argentina has more than 100 radio stations and numerous television stations. Buenos Aires alone has four television stations—three are state-owned, and one is private. It is estimated that there is one radio for every 1.5 Argentines and one television set for every 5.2 Argentines. In comparison, the averages for the United States are two radios per person and one television per 1.7 persons. Argentine viewers watch television programs imported from the United States and dubbed in Spanish.

EDUCATION AND LITERACY

Argentina has an impressive 96 percent literacy rate. Education is free from kindergarten to university. Most children attend seven grades of elementary school, even in rural areas where there are fewer schools.

Education is compulsory for all children in Argentina.

The school year runs from March to December in most parts of the country. Lessons are taught in Spanish; English, French, and Italian are taught as second languages. Elementary school students may wear white coats over their own clothes. In many junior high schools, the students wear uniforms.

Although secondary education is not compulsory, there are free government schools in addition to private schools, in most big towns and cities. These offer five-year programs. Only a small percentage of students finish secondary school.

There are more than 50 public and private universities. The University of Buenos Aires is the largest, with more than 100,000 students. Founded in 1613, the University of Córdoba is the nation's oldest. Because many students work full-time, night courses are quite popular. The three most popular majors are architecture, political science, and medicine.

Public schools largely owe their success to President Domingo Faustino Sarmiento (1811–1888), who enlisted the advice of famous American educator Horace Mann to help set up the public school system. However, Argentina's school system is modeled closely after the French system. In the 1800s, schools helped immigrant children adapt to Argentine society.

PROVERBS WITH A SPANISH TWIST

Proverbs take on a different flavor in different languages. Here are some English proverbs and their Spanish counterparts translated in English:

- Too many cooks spoil the broth.
  Spanish: A ship directed by many captains soon sinks.
- Don't count your chickens before they're hatched.
  Spanish: Don't eat the sausages before you kill the pig.
- A bird in the hand is worth two in the bush.
  Spanish: A bird in the hand is worth a hundred flying.
- You cannot make a silk purse out of a sow's ear.
  Spanish: You can't find pears on an elm'tree.
- Much ado about nothing.
  Spanish: Much noise (of cracking), few nuts.

(Sources: *Native Tongues* by Charles Berlitz and *La Illustración Argentina.*)

ARTS

IF THE HEART of Argentina is its people, the soul of the country is its artistic culture. Argentine artists have excelled in a variety of fields, including music, dance, literature, architecture, painting, and sculpture.

Argentina's creative capital is the multicultural Buenos Aires region. *Porteño* art takes its inspiration from the kaleidoscope of cultures that have settled in the greater Buenos Aires area over the years. Predominantly European in style, *porteño* art has, nonetheless, developed its own distinctive Argentine character. Today, Buenos Aires is a thriving cultural center, boasting fine museums and art galleries, world-famous opera houses, and a number of theaters. The city's symphony orchestra, dance companies, and theater groups are established and well-known abroad. Other large cities also house libraries, museums, theaters, and concert halls.

Opposite: **The passionate tango is the most famous artistic form to have come out of Argentina.**

Below: **Outdoor art stalls selling a variety of paintings abound in Argentina.**

The power of Argentine artists has survived despite periods of great political repression. Some writers were forced to go into exile, while others courageously chose to stay and continue their work at home. The return of democracy to Argentina in the 1980s sparked a revival in the arts.

Unlike in most other Latin American countries, indigenous arts in Argentina have had little influence on the overall development of the country's artistic culture. Still, indigenous Argentines do produce woodcarvings, bolas, *yerba mate* sets, jewelry, and other handicrafts that exhibit a blend of Indian and Spanish traditions.

ART THROUGH ARGENTINE EYES

INDIGENOUS ART The oldest works of art found in Argentina are cave paintings and engravings. Small stone heads and a carving of a human foot with six toes have also been found.

The archaeological remains and pre-Columbian menhirs—tall stone columns—in Tafí del Valle in Tucumán Province are particularly striking. Tall standing stones, some 10 feet (3 m) high, have been collected in Menhir Park. Scholars cannot agree on their age or the meaning of their inscriptions.

The Diaguita, an indigenous group, created circles of engraved stones. Dozens of these stones remain in Tafí del Valle, a valley sacred to the Diaguita.

Prehistoric ceramics of the Condorhuasi culture are known by their strange shapes, with animal and human characteristics.

COLONIAL AND POST-INDEPENDENCE ART After the arrival of the Spanish and throughout colonial times, religious themes dominated the country's artistic scene. Manuel Belgrano founded the School of Geometry, Perspective and Drawing in Buenos Aires during the colonial period.

Prilidiano Pueyrredón and Cándido López dominated Argentina's 19th-century art scene. Carlos Morel and Fernando García Molina are painters who became famous in the 1830s. In more recent times, Benito Quinquela Martín and Uruguayan-born Pedro Figari have depicted life in present-day Buenos Aires.

Lucio Fontana and Fernando Arranz are well known for their work in ceramics. The sculptures of Julio le Parc and Alicia Peñalba are widely known within and beyond Argentina. Photographer Pedro Luis Raota has won awards in at least 22 countries.

Modern Argentine artists have reverted to creating works of art for the sake of their artistic value, rather than to make political criticism or social commentary. Some artists have blurred the distinction between photography, painting, and sculpture. The visual and dramatic arts are sometimes combined in performance pieces.

The works of Argentine artists can be admired in over 100 art galleries in Buenos Aires as well as in the numerous galleries and museums found in the smaller cities.

Opposite top: **Indian handicrafts. Although Argentina's indigenous civilizations did not reach the artistic height of the Incas in Peru, they did produce beautiful and artistic crafts.**

Opposite bottom: **In the larger cities, sculptures and murals are displayed in public for everyone to see.**

Below: **A wall mural—street art is very popular in Argentina.**

GAUCHO ART

Gaucho accessories. Beautifully-crafted spurs, knife cases, bolas, and leather belts were used by the *gauchos* in their daily tasks.

The *gaucho* has inspired Argentine literature, painting, and music. His rugged, courageous, and rustic way of life is seen as embodying the ideal lifestyle of an Argentine.

However, the *gaucho* was not always regarded as the romantic hero he is today. President Domingo Sarmiento (1868–1874) attacked the legend of the proud, rebellious *gaucho* in *Civilization and Barbarism: Life of Juan Facundo Quiroga* (1845). Sarmiento felt that education, not rebellion, was the key to the country's future. *El Gaucho Martin Fierro* (1872), an epic poem by José Hernández, changed this view of the *gaucho*. Describing in vivid detail the difficult life of a *gaucho*, this poem is considered a literary masterpiece. As Argentina's "national poem," it is still read in schools. Hernández's portrait was sympathetic to the plight of the *gauchos*. He portrayed the people they often fought with—indigenous Indians, Afro-Argentines, the military, and the police—and depicted the forces that threatened the *gaucho* way of life.

Novelists influenced by Hernández include Benito Lynch and Ricardo Güiraldes. Güiraldes' *Don Segundo Sombra* (1926) imaginatively portrayed the decline of the *gaucho*. A group of young writers in the 1920s, known as the *Martinfierristas*, published a literary review called *Martín Fierro*. World-famous writer Jorge Luis Borges was a member of this group.

The father of Argentine national music, Alberto Williams, composed a piece called *Aires de la Pampa* inspired by *gaucho* life in 1893.

THE WRITTEN WORD

Many Argentine writers first came to the attention of the outside world when their works were published in the literary magazine *Sur*. The magazine was founded in 1931 by Victoria Ocampo, a rich, aristocratic writer. She also published short stories and poems by foreign writers in Spanish translation, introducing foreign literature to the Argentine public.

The most famous Argentine writers of the last century include Jorge Luis Borges, Leopoldo Lugones, Manuel Ugarte, Alfredo Palacios, Ernesto Sábato, Julio Cortázar, Manuel Puig, and Adolfo Bioy-Casares.

Bioy-Casares wrote a chronicle of *porteño* life called *Asleep in the Sun*, among other books. He also collaborated with Jorge Luis Borges on several books, published under a common pseudonym. Cortázar is known for his short stories and novels, such as *Rayuela*, and his works have been translated into many languages.

A secondhand bookshop in Buenos Aires, where book-loving Argentines can buy books for a fraction of their original price.

Celeste Goes Dancing is an engaging sample in English translation of stories written in the 1980s by 14 representative Argentine writers.

Jacobo Timmerman, a newspaper editor, gained international recognition with his book *Prisoner Without a Name, Cell Without a Number* (1981). After being treated brutally by the military authorities, Timmerman accused them of attacking him not only because he had expressed dissent against the government but also because he was a Jew.

JORGE LUIS BORGES (1899–1986)

Probably the most famous of Argentine writers, Jorge Luis Borges wrote essays, poetry, and short stories that inspired an entire generation of writers. Borges was admired for his brilliant use of language and his original thoughts about the meaning of life and other philosophical questions. His stories, which critics have compared to the stories of Edgar Allan Poe, convey a sense of mystery and fantasy.

Borges' international outlook on literature may have sprung from his family roots. His father was of Italian, Jewish, and English heritage, while his mother was of Argentine and Uruguayan heritage. Borges studied in Switzerland and published his first poem in Spain. He disapproved of Perón but took no active part in politics. In 1927, Borges began to lose his vision and was completely blind by the age of 56. With the help of assistants, books and writing remained the passion of his life. At 68, he wed for the first time, but the marriage did not last. Shortly before his death, he married his 41-year-old assistant.

Among Borges' best-known books available in English are *Ficciones* (Fictions) and *El Aleph* ("aleph" is the first letter of the Hebrew alphabet). Borges won many literary honors, including Spain's most important literary award, the Cervantes Prize, in 1980. He was nominated for the Nobel Prize, but never won it.

Opposite top: **The most famous tango singer of all time, Carlos Gardel. Gardel's music is as popular today as it was during his lifetime.**

Opposite bottom: **A pair of tango dancers strikes a dramatic pose.**

MUSIC AND DANCE

Composers in Argentina have been influenced by both European and *gaucho* music. In the 17th century, Jesuit missionaries taught music to the indigenous Indians as a form of evangelism. Amancio Alcorta (1805–1862) is considered to be Argentina's first local-born composer. His main works include waltzes, polkas, and other kinds of dance music. Born to a wealthy family in Santiago del Estero, Alcorta served in Argentina's senate.

Italian immigrants gave Argentina a taste for opera. Today, opera is second only to the tango in popularity. More than 70 Argentine operas have been produced at home and abroad. Alberto Ginastera's opera *Bomarzo* is remembered for its violent theme and its dramatic impact on audiences.

Folk dancing thrives in provinces such as Salta. Dance styles resemble Incan, Spanish, *gaucho*, and other Latin American forms of dancing.

ARGENTINA'S TANGO The passionate tango is Argentina's most famous cultural contribution to the world. As a dance, the tango is performed by a couple holding each other tightly and gliding together in long, elegant steps, occasionally pausing in dramatic poses. The accompanying lyrics are often a melancholic musing on lost love.

The tango appeared in the late 1800s and gained worldwide popularity in the early 1900s. Some scholars trace its roots to gypsy music in Spain, while others say it developed from the *milonga* ("mee-LOHN-gah")—an earlier dance popular in Argentina—and other dances such as the polka. Tango music is generally played by guitar, violin, flute, piano, and especially *bandoneón* ("bahn-doh-NYOHN"), an instrument similar to the accordion. People who dance the tango are called tango interpreters.

Originating in the working class, the tango was at first considered vulgar by the upper class. In the 1920s, the pope declared that dancing the tango was not a sin. Its popularity then spread to the upper classes in Buenos Aires and to other countries around the world. The tango is now performed mostly for tourists.

MUSEUMS AND SCIENTISTS

The National Museum of Fine Arts, opened in Buenos Aires in 1896, is becoming a showcase for the works of local artists. Today the museum houses works by modern Argentine and foreign artists as well as 400-year-old paintings illustrating Argentina's early history.

Other museums in Buenos Aires include the Museum of Spanish-American Art, with its valuable collection of colonial artifacts and silver pieces, and the Pharmacy Museum, where antiques from old pharmacies are on display. The José Hernández Museum specializes in the culture of the *gauchos*. The city of Rosario has an excellent Museum of Modern Art. Founded in 1877, the Natural Science Museum in La Plata has a world-famous fossil collection. Many of the fossils were discovered by Florentino Ameghino (1854-1911), one of the world's first paleontologists, in the *pampas* and in Patagonia.

FILM

Argentina's movie industry developed after World War I. Buenos Aires and Mexico City became Latin America's main film-making capitals from the 1930s to the 1950s.

Argentine movies have won awards in film festivals around the world. In the United States, *The Official Story* won an Oscar for Best Foreign Film in 1985. Actress Norma Aleandro was nominated for Best Actress in that film. She portrayed a woman who discovers that her adopted daughter is the child of one of the "disappeared." *Kiss of the Spider Woman,* a film based on Argentine Manuel Puig's novel, also depicted the government's persecution of the people. Actor William Hurt won the Academy Award for Best Actor in that film in 1986. Although the local film-making industry is thriving, movies imported from the United States and Europe are still the most popular among Argentines.

Streets in Argentina are filled with movie posters, which advertise an array of U.S., European, and local films.

Built in 1613, Córdoba University is Argentina's oldest university and a beautiful example of colonial architecture.

The Teatro Colón is one of the world's largest and most elegant opera houses. Built between 1887 and 1908, it is considered the finest concert hall in Latin America.

ARCHITECTURE

Colonial buildings are well-preserved in northern Argentina, where the first Spanish settlers built the country's oldest towns. Córdoba's cathedral, completed in 1784, is a beautiful example of colonial architecture. Following Spanish practice, the cathedral faces a plaza, or open square. In the countryside, many lavish estates were built in the colonial style.

The buildings in Buenos Aires display Spanish and Italian influences, but visitors feel the city resembles Paris the most. Wide boulevards, apartment buildings with charming balconies, and large government buildings dating from the 1800s remind many visitors of the French capital. Numerous parks and gardens, many exhibiting marble statues and fountains, add to the beauty of the city.

BENITO QUINQUELA MARTÍN AND LA BOCA

If an artist could change the look of a city, painter Benito Quinquela Martín (1890–1977) was the right person for the job. He first built a primary school for the poor children of La Boca, formerly a slum area of Buenos Aires. When he handed the school to the city, it was on the condition that the school also house a museum of waterfront paintings. As a result, La Boca became an art neighborhood, with Quinquela as one of its most famous artists.

Quinquela persuaded a number of restaurant owners in La Boca to paint their buildings in bright colors. Owners of run-down homes in the neighborhood followed suit, painting them in vivid reds, yellows, and blues. Quinquela also established an open-air market to promote the work of local artists.

The river-front section of La Boca remains a favorite gathering spot for artists and poets. Tourists enjoy the view of the colorful buildings. Nostalgic music pouring out of clubs brings visitors back in time to when the tango was first played in the dance halls of La Boca.

LEISURE

THE ARGENTINE CLIMATE favors outdoor activities throughout the year. The name Buenos Aires, or "Good Winds," comes from the early Spaniards' gratitude to the Virgin of the Good Winds for their safe arrival in this land. Argentines still enjoy good winds and fresh air near beautiful lakes and rivers, the Atlantic Ocean, and the Andes Mountains. These places boast ideal conditions for camping, hunting, fishing, hiking, mountain climbing, skiing, sailing, windsurfing, and cycling. Argentines also take vacations in resort areas such as Bariloche.

Team sports attract many Argentines, both players and spectators. Besides soccer, the national sport, other sports such as basketball, cricket, polo, and rugby are extremely popular in Argentina. Fans heartily cheer their favorite teams and players during playoffs and final matches. Argentines have been known to celebrate a favorite team's victory with festivities that last for days.

Following *gaucho* tradition, Argentines in the *pampas* like rugged contests on horseback. Unlike in many other Spanish-speaking countries, however, bullfighting is not popular in Argentina.

Opposite: **Enthusiastic crowds gather to support their favorite soccer team at a match between Boca Juniors and River Plate—Argentina's most popular soccer teams—at La Boca Stadium.**

Below: **Children play near the rock pools of Iguazú Falls.**

A PASSION FOR SOCCER

The most popular sport in Argentina is soccer, or *fútbol* ("FOOT-bohl") in Spanish. The English brought this game to Argentina in the 19th century.

Children grow up playing soccer at school, in the street, or in any open space. Competition to be selected for a prestigious team is fierce. Boys who manage to become professional soccer players can expect to earn big salaries. Star players often become national heroes.

The dream of every Argentine boy is to become a soccer star.

In Buenos Aires, a traditional rivalry exists between the Boca Juniors team from the Italian neighborhood of La Boca and the River Plate team. Three-quarters of the nation's soccer fans support one of these two teams.

Among national teams, a passionate rivalry exists between Argentina and Brazil. In the past, more than 100,000 fans have turned out to watch individual games between the two countries.

Some of Argentina's best soccer players are recruited to play for famous foreign clubs, particularly in Europe. Brazil and Mexico also hire Argentine players. However, these soccer stars often return home to play for Argentina's national team in the World Cup games.

Argentina's long list of honors in its soccer history include winning the Junior World Championship in 1979 and the World Cup in 1978 and 1986. In the 1990 World Cup championship, after defeating Brazil and host country Italy, Argentina lost to West Germany in the final. Nevertheless, Sergio Goycochea, the substitute goalkeeper who stepped in during the final matches, became a national hero due to his superb and inspirational performance on the field.

Argentina's greatest soccer star, Diego Maradona, and his teammates celebrate their winning goal against Brazil in a 1990 World Cup match.

SMALL BUT MIGHTY

A few years ago, Argentina's Diego Armando Maradona was considered the best soccer player in the world. His fiery personality, tremendous athletic skill, and superb performances have made him the subject of many stories. The 5-foot-5-inch (1.65-m) star from the poor Villa Fiorito slum in Buenos Aires has earned a variety of nicknames, from "golden boy" and "king of soccer" to "Mr. Disagreeable." Maradona sported No. 10 on his jersey, the number traditionally given to a team's best scorer. Soccer's greatest star, Pele, also wore No. 10. Much like Pele's story, Maradona's life is also a rags-to-riches story.

Maradona has played for teams on both sides of the Atlantic. He played for Italy's Napoli club and led Argentina's team in three World Cups, including their most recent win in 1986. Since the early 1990s, Maradona has had a rocky relationship with drug abuse. He was twice suspended from playing for using illegal drugs and finally retired from the field in 1997. In 1998 he traveled with the Argentine national team to comment on the World Cup and is currently negotiating to coach the 2002 team.

The game of polo, like soccer, was brought to Argentina by British immigrants in the 1800s.

BRITISH HORSEBACK

The game of polo, played on specially-bred ponies, was brought to Argentina by British immigrants. Drawing on their *gaucho* tradition of great horsemanship, Argentines quickly took to the game.

In Buenos Aires, crowds of 20,000 people routinely turn out to cheer for their favorite players. Gonzalo Pieres, a national polo hero, is also ranked as one of the world's best.

Polo players begin their training as children, swinging little mallets from bicycles. They then join polo leagues to compete against other teams. Argentina's best polo players usually come from families that own large farms. Players can practice year-round on the farm. Family teams of fathers, sons, uncles, and cousins are common. Prized for their speed and ability to work with their riders, Argentine polo ponies are some of the most expensive of their type in the world.

Show-jumping is another sport which has given local riders international recognition. The National Polo Fields and the Argentine Horsetrack are located in the suburb of Palermo. As Argentines love to attend horse races, a new race track has been built in the Buenos Aires suburb of San Isidro.

GAUCHO HORSEBACK

The horseback game of *pato* ("PAH-toh") originated with the *gauchos*. *Pato* was originally played using a live duck (*pato* is Spanish for "duck"). The duck was placed in a sack with its head sticking out. Two teams would race over a 3-mile-long (4.8-km-long) field fighting over the sack. As the games often ended in violent, bloody fights, the local government banned *pato* in 1822. The game was legalized again under President Juan Manuel de Rosas. Today, a six-handled, inflated leather bag has replaced the duck. To score points, players must land the bag in a netted iron hoop 3 feet (91 cm) in diameter at the opponent's end of the playing field. *Pato* has traditionally been a working-class game, but its popularity has spread to other social groups. As in polo, *pato* horses are valued for their speed, strength, endurance, and ability to work with their riders.

In the game of *sortija* ("sor-TEE-ha"), a horseman gallops at full speed and tries to lance a small ring, or *sortija*, hanging from a bar. Much skill is needed, as the ring may be as tiny as a wedding ring.

Rodeos are popular in many parts of Argentina. Descendants of the traditional *gauchos* demonstrate their skills in roping and riding contests. The most important rodeo is held each May in Ayacucho.

Opposite: **Juan Fangio.**

RACING LEGEND JUAN FANGIO

Like soccer star Diego Armando Maradona, Juan Manuel Fangio (1911–1995) was born in poverty but acquired international fame and wealth through competitive sports.

In the 1950s, racing star Fangio won the Grand Prix championship five times. The lives of racing drivers then were glamorous but risky. Drivers wore neither hard helmets nor flame-proof clothing. Thirty drivers—all of them Fangio's friends—died in flaming wrecks at the prime of their careers in that decade alone. Although not a rarity today, fatal race track accidents have become less common than in the past. This is due in no small part to technological advances in automobile safety features, such as better brakes and wider tires.

In his autobiography, Fangio devoted an entire chapter to the topic of luck. Fangio's belief was that "no one dies before a day that is marked." He also said that "whenever someone was killed, I thought to myself, surely he committed an error." Due to such remarks, he was accused of being cold-blooded. In fact, old newsreels show him driving skillfully past burning wrecks, as they rolled into screaming spectators. Fangio trusted his skills, his mechanics, and his cars. He had two accidents in which his co-driver died. Fangio later blamed those crashes on his lack of sleep.

Fangio grew up in a poor family and, as a child, worked long hours in a garage. Perhaps it was there that he gained his legendary ability to communicate with the engines and tires of his cars. On his first race, in 1929, he drove a Ford taxi but later won races driving Alfa Romeos, Mercedes-Benzes, Ferraris, and Maseratis. After his retirement, at the top of his career, Fangio became president of Mercedes-Benz in South America. He founded a museum in his hometown of Balcarce, where 500 of his trophies and 50 of his racing and classic cars are on display.

SCALING THE HEIGHTS

Every year, in early August, Bariloche hosts a snow carnival and the annual national ski championship.

Mountain climbers from around the world come to Argentina to attempt to reach the tops of the Andes peaks. Mendoza, about 800 miles (1,290 km) west of Buenos Aires, is Argentina's most popular spot for mountain

climbing. Mt. Aconcagua, the highest peak in the Western Hemisphere, poses a challenge to expert climbers. Matias Zurbriggen from Switzerland was the first to reach the summit of Mt. Aconcagua in 1897. There are ten recognized routes up the mountain, but most climbers use the northern route.

Teams from Germany, Italy, Switzerland, and the United States have attempted to climb Mt. Aconcagua. Over the years, the peak has claimed many lives; climbers that die on the mountain are usually buried in a small cemetery at its foot.

Hang gliding is also popular in Argentina. The sport is sponsored by the nation's Air Force. International competitions are held in the hills near Córdoba, an area famous for challenging wind drafts.

SPORTS HEROES

Argentina has produced many sports heroes. While Juan Fangio won the world championship races five times, other Argentines such as Carlos Alberto Reutemann—a famous Grand Prix driver—and Ricardo Zunino have quickly followed his tracks.

The most famous Argentine boxer is probably Luis Angel Firpo, who fought in the 1920s. He was called "the wild bull of the pampas" and is honored with a statue in Buenos Aires. He knocked world heavyweight champion Jack Dempsey out of the ring in 1923, but lost the match. Other Argentine boxers have been world champions in various categories. Carlos Monzón held the middleweight title from 1970 to 1977.

Argentina's international tennis stars include Guillermo Vilas, José Luis Clerc, Ivanna Madruga, and Gabriela Sabatini. In 1983, at the age of 13, Sabatini became the youngest player to win the Orange Bowl trophy for players under 18 years of age.

Rugby star Hugo Porta, who made his debut in 1971, is considered one of the greatest players of all time. He later served as Argentina's ambassador to South Africa and as the country's sports secretary.

Argentina has also produced a number of outstanding swimmers. In 1962, at the age of 17, Luis Alberto Nicolao broke the world record in the 100-m butterfly style. More recently, José Meolans placed second in the 100-m swimming competition at the Goodwill Games held in Australia.

Fishing championships are held in Bariloche each year. A record 36-pound (16-kg) trout was caught in that region. Competitions are also held each year in Paso de la Patria, a town on the Paraná River in the northeast. People compete to catch the largest golden dorado, a fighting fish that can weigh up to 60 pounds (27 kg).

In 1978, Argentina won the world championship ice hockey title.

By the time he retired from racing in 1959, Juan Fangio had won 16 world championship Grand Prix races, including four consecutive German title races.

FESTIVALS

WHEN ARGENTINA COMES ALIVE with festivals, or *fiestas* ("fee-EHS-tahs"), colorful parades brighten the landscape from one end of the country to the other. Argentines in different parts of the country express their artistic, musical, and culinary creativity through festivals that reflect indigenous and Christian traditions. Some festivals commemorate historical events. For example, each city celebrates the anniversary of its founding. In other festivals, people celebrate the legends and traditions of the many cultures that have enriched Argentina's history.

Argentine festivals and holidays may involve religious pilgrimages, feasts, parades, dancing, and sometimes *gaucho* horseback competitions. Most of the competitors in horseback events are descendants of the traditional *gauchos*. They use old costumes and saddles for the contest. The Gaucho Festival of San Antonio de Areco, 80 miles (128 km) north of Buenos Aires, takes place from November 10 to November 17.

Opposite: **Santa Claus in Buenos Aires. Christmas, which falls in the middle of summer, is widely celebrated in Argentina.**

Below: **Guards parade in front of the Casa Rosada, the government palace.**

The traditions of immigrant communities form the basis for some Argentine festivals. The Welsh singing festival takes place in October in Trevelin, a Patagonian mountain town near Esquel. A gathering of Welsh musicians and poets also takes place each year at Gaiman in Patagonia.

WINE, MATE, WHEAT, AND PONCHOS

Some Argentine festivals celebrate the chief agricultural products of a region. In Mendoza, the winemaking area along the Andes, the Vendimia Festival is celebrated in March to mark the grape harvest. Honoring more than 1,500 wine producers from the region, it is one of the most impressive festivals in Latin America. The vines are blessed in a special ceremony, fountains of red wine are free for the crowd to taste, a festival queen is chosen, and a magnificent parade is held. The people of Mendoza also celebrate their history. At the end of February, before the wine festival begins, they commemorate General San Martín's crossing of the Andes.

In Posadas, the capital of the province of Misiones, the people hold an annual festival to celebrate the harvest of *mate*, a holly brewed to make *yerba mate*, the national drink. Ornately-decorated coaches carrying young ladies from every district of the province parade through the streets of Posadas, and one of the girls is chosen as the year's *mate* queen.

The most important wheat festival in Argentina takes place in Leones in the province of Córdoba. A wheat queen is chosen at the commercial and industrial fair, and a number of folkloric events are celebrated. People in the central farming province of La Pampa also celebrate harvest festivals.

The Fiesta del Poncho in Catamarca features the local production of hand-woven ponchos. The fleece for these garments comes from three animals that live high in the Andes Mountains—the alpaca, the llama, and the vicuña. The people of Catamarca proudly display their ponchos as the symbol of a continuing ancient tradition. For the *gauchos,* ponchos were an indispensable piece of clothing that protected them from the cold and strong winds of the *pampas.*

On May 25, people dress in costumes and masks reminiscent of the early 19th century to celebrate the day when Argentina declared itself independent from Spain in 1810.

CARNIVAL

Carnival is a festivity often celebrated in Catholic countries around the world. Mardi Gras in the United States is a celebration that originated in Carnival festivities. The celebration of Carnival in Argentina is particularly lavish in the northern part of the country. Business comes to a halt as Argentines dressed in outrageous costumes dance in the streets.

Carnival festivities begin on the weekend before Ash Wednesday, which usually falls in February. In the northeast, the celebrations are mixed with Indian traditions. In Tilcara, floral arrangements representing the stations of the cross are hung along the streets, and processions come down the mountains on Ash Wednesday.

Carnival in Argentina is not celebrated with the same abandon as it is in Brazil. Visitors, however, may find that many Argentines are often attending parties and that business is interrupted during Carnival. Typical ways of celebrating include holding drinking parties till the early hours of the morning and drenching one another with water balloons. Hotels and clubs in major cities hold parties during Carnival.

Carnival celebrations in Argentina usually begin in the early evening and last until the early hours of the morning.

REGIONAL FESTIVALS

A colorful regional festival takes place somewhere in Argentina almost every month of the year. In Puerto Madryn, an underwater fishing festival kicks off the New Year. In Rosario del Tala, a Tango Festival runs through the first half of January. The last half of January is devoted to a two-week National Folklore Festival in Cosquín in the province of Córdoba. An artisan fair is held in Cosquín at almost the same time.

On February 2, processions on horseback at Humahuaca near Jujuy bring pilgrims to the Candelaria Virgin. Fireworks, traditional foods, and religious music add to the celebrations. Northern Argentines meet with southern Bolivians during Easter week to trade handicrafts and other goods. They also meet on the last two Sundays of October at the *Manca Fiesta*, or Festival of the Pot, where trading takes place.

Salta Week, starting on June 14, marks the anniversary of a local battle. While San Martín was fighting the Spanish, Salta's town hero, General

Martín Miguel de Güemes, led a band of *gauchos* against the Spanish in the Gaucho War. This festival includes fireworks, colorful floats, singing, and dancing. Salta is also noted for its Christmas performances, tableaus, and caroling, which continue for weeks.

Corrientes, which has a particularly lively Carnival celebration, marks its founding on May 3 with a religious and popular arts festival.

On June 24, St. John's Day is celebrated in several towns. In Formosa, the faithful walk barefoot over a bed of hot coals. Every year, on July 25, processions in Salta, Jujuy, and Mendoza honor St. James. St. Ann is honored a day later in Tilcara, near Jujuy.

Also in July, Argentines gather at the annual Livestock Exhibition at the Argentine Rural Society in Buenos Aires. Cattle, horses, sheep, and pigs are judged for prizes and sold at auctions.

Reenacting historical events and holding military parades are two popular ways Argentines celebrate and remember their history.

The small village of Villa General Belgrano hosts an Alpine Chocolate Festival every winter as well as an authentic Oktoberfest, or German beer festival.

Thousands of Catholic believers make a pilgrimage several times a year to celebrate the Fiesta of our Lady of Luján, the patron saint of Argentina. Many make the journey from their homes to Luján on foot. Early in December, old coaches from a colonial museum in Luján parade around town as part of the festivities.

MUSICAL CELEBRATIONS

The northwest of Argentina is the region with the oldest history of Spanish settlement. At the same time, it remains the heart of indigenous Indian culture. The region's history has contributed to unique musical celebrations that blend both Indian and Spanish traditions.

Argentine folk music is performed mainly by Argentines from the northwestern region of the country, near Bolivia.

Traditional Indian customs are preserved through colorful celebrations, such as the *misachicos* ("mee-sah-CHEE-kos"), the carnival of Jujuy, and other religious festivals.

On these occasions, musicians come down from the mountains to crowd the narrow, steep streets of the colonial villages. They bring with them *erkes* ("EHR-kes"), long trumpets that make a loud, distinctive sound audible from a distance; *charangos* ("chah-RAHN-gos"), small guitars made from the carcasses of local armadillo; and typical bass drums.

The joyful music of indigenous Argentines comes to life in these celebrations. *Carnavalitos* ("kahr-nah-vah-LEE-tohs"), *bagualas* ("bah-goo-AH-lahs"), *zambas* ("SAHM-bahs"), *cuecas* ("koo-EH-kahs"), and *chacareras* ("chah-kah-RAY-rahs") are some local musical tunes. They are sometimes played with indigenous instruments like *erkes, charangos*, bass drums, *bombos* ("BOHM-bohs"), *sikus* ("SEE-koos"), and *quenas* ("KAY-nahs"); other times, they are also played with European instruments, such as guitars, violins, and large accordions.

TWO INDEPENDENCE DAYS

The long-standing rivalry between the people of Buenos Aires and the people of the provinces has resulted in Argentines celebrating two independence days.

May 25 marks the date when the people of Buenos Aires declared independence from Spain. The people of the provinces celebrate the holiday on July 9, when deputies of the interior Congress of Tucumán declared the United Provinces free. Today, people in the capital and countryside celebrate both holidays.

During the May 25 celebrations, a lavish parade is held. The Plaza de Mayo is filled with army officers in riding boots, naval officers in 19th-century frock coats and spats, and soldiers massed in battle gear and black berets, in a reenactment of the struggle for nationhood. As the proud symbol of Argentina, the regal *gauchos* ride on horseback, their red cloaks flowing in the wind.

PUBLIC HOLIDAYS

Official public holidays include both religious and historical celebrations.

January 1	New Year's Day
January 6	Epiphany
March/April	Maundy Thursday, Good Friday, and Easter Sunday
May 1	Labor Day
May 25	Anniversary of the Revolution of 1810
June 10	Malvinas Day, commemorating the Falklands War
June 20	Flag Day
July 9	Independence Day
August 17	Anniversary of the death of General José de San Martín, the liberator of Argentina
October 12	Columbus Day
December 8	Catholic feast of the Immaculate Conception
December 25	Christmas

FOOD

AN ARGENTINE SAYING goes that every Argentine is an expert at barbecuing; and no wonder, since beef is by far the most popular food, and some Argentines eat it three times a day.

Traditionally, meat was spit-roasted in the courtyard of the home or in the fields. It was often pierced through a cross-shaped spit, one end of which was driven into the ground at an angle to keep the roast over the flames. At other times, it was cooked on a grill over hot coals.

Today, the average Argentine consumes 190 pounds (86 kg) of beef per year. Writers have attributed the overwhelming popularity of beef to a belief that eating it gives people the animal's vitality and that people must eat plenty of it to be strong. Perhaps the real reason why so much beef is consumed is that it is plentiful and cheap. Many people consider Argentine beef the best in the world, tender enough to be cut with a fork.

A typical meal consists of grilled beef with French fries, salad, and red wine. In restaurants, beef is served in hearty portions. Some restaurants place a small stove at each table and barbecue the meats in front of their customers. The meat is usually seasoned before it reaches the table.

It is not unusual for someone in the office to take a trip to the butcher's a little before lunchtime to buy some fresh meat to be roasted or grilled for his or her colleagues to have for lunch.

Argentines are slowly absorbing the news that eating less red meat may lower cholesterol levels and improve health. Still, grilled beef remains the favorite food among Argentines.

Opposite: **A waiter serves snacks and bottles of wine. Most Argentines drink wine with their meals.**

Below: **Meat is so popular in Argentina that whole animals are barbecued over an open fire.**

ARGENTINE MEALS

Aside from the predictable main course, side dishes can also have an Argentine flair. *Matambre* ("mah-TAHM-breh"), meaning "hunger killer," is an appetizer of baked marinated flank steak stuffed with spinach, hearts of palm, and ham or hard-boiled eggs. It can be eaten hot or cold.

Lettuce and tomato salads are tossed with oil—often olive oil—and vinegar or lemon juice. The creamy and cheesy salad dressings of the United States are rare in Argentina.

Desserts include fresh fruit and cheese and the much-loved *dulce de leche* ("DOOL-seh de LAy-cheh")—milk simmered with sugar until it thickens. This sweet concoction is used as a filling in other desserts.

Alfajores con dulce de leche is a pastry with two layers of dough and a filling, coated with powdered sugar. Each region of the country has its own style. For chocolate lovers, chocolate versions are plentiful and delicious. *Dulce de leche* is also spread on breakfast toast, eaten by the spoonful, served along with ice cream, and used in cakes and meringues. Sometimes it is eaten with cheese to cut its sweetness.

Rice pudding and *almendrado* ("ahl-mehn-DRAH-doh"), ice cream rolled in crushed almonds, also satisfy the Argentine sweet tooth. Italian-style ice creams abound throughout Argentina.

INDIGENOUS FOOD

One of the few truly indigenous dishes in Argentina is *locro* ("LAW-kroh"), a thick corn stew. *Locro* contains beef, beans, potatoes, peppers, onions, and ingredients typical of the Andes.

The indigenous Indian influence on food is most noticeable in the north. In the northeast, near the famous Iguazú Falls, typical dishes created by the Guaraní include *chipa* ("CHEE-pah"), a small, hard biscuit made of manioc, eggs, and cheese.

Sopa paraguaya ("SOH-pah pah-rah-WAH-zhah") is a pie made of corn, cheese, and eggs. *Reviro* ("reh-VEE-roh") is a breakfast dish made of milk, flour, eggs, and cheese.

In the northwest, certain dishes reflect *mestizo* heritage. *Huminta en chala* ("oo-MEEN-tah ehn CHAH-lah") is a mildly spicy cornmeal tamale cooked in corn husks.

Sweets and candies of all shapes and colors are sold at streetside stalls.

123

INTERNATIONAL INFLUENCE

The food of Argentina is really a blend of Italian, Jewish, Spanish, Polish, and German foods. Only the indigenous Indian dishes originated in Argentina. Contemporary Argentine cuisine reflects the different ethnic groups that immigrated and settled in the country.

The *gauchos* contributed the *asado* ("ah-SAH-doh"), beef roasted over an open wood or coal fire. *Bife a caballo* ("BEE-feh ah kah-VAH-zhoh"), or "beef on horseback,"is a steak topped with fried eggs; *carbonada* ("kar-boh-NAH-dah") is a stew made with beef, corn, squash, and peaches and baked in a pumpkin shell; *churrasco* ("choor-RAHS-koh") is grilled steak; *chorizos* ("choh-REE-sohs") are spicy sausages; and *morcillas* ("mohr-SEE-zhas") are blood sausages popular in German and Polish cooking.

At the *parrillada* ("par-ree-ZHAH-da"), a grill house that cooks meats over charcoal fires, one can order a *parrillada mixta,* or mixed grill. Some Argentines enjoy grilling an assortment of sausages, short ribs, and organ meats, such as kidneys, liver, and sweetbreads, and even cow's udders.

From Italy comes the *milanesa* ("mee-lah-NEH-sah"), thinly-sliced beef coated with beaten egg and bread crumbs, then deep-fried. Spanish cooking inspired *puchero de gallina* ("poo-CHEH-roh day gah-ZHEE-nah"), a chicken stew made with corn, sausages, potatoes, and squash. Children like *ñoquis* ("NYOH-kees"), potato dumplings served with meat and tomato sauce. Argentine *empanadas* ("ehm-pah-NAH-dahs") derive from Britain's Cornish pastries. They are fried or baked crescent-shaped pastries, stuffed with chopped meats, cheese, creamed corn, fish or seafood. Chopped hardboiled eggs, olives, and onions are sometimes used to flavor the filling.

FINDING FOOD

Eating out is a favorite activity in Argentina. There are many types of restaurants and shops that cater to the fussiest of diners. The great majority of restaurants feature beef. Some can seat hundreds of people and are open 24 hours a day. People may linger for hours over a three-course meal, and some restaurants hire orchestras to entertain diners.

Sidewalk cafés line the wide boulevards of Buenos Aires. Argentines take advantage of a moderate climate to enjoy English tea in the afternoon at outdoor tables.

The names of food shops sound like poetry—*pizzerías (“pee-tseh-REE-ahs”)*; *cafeterías (“kah-feh-teh-REE-ahs”)*; *heladerías (“eh-lah-deh-REE-ahs”)*, which serve ice cream; and *confiterías* (“kohn-fee-teh-REE-ahs”), which serve cakes, sandwiches, *empanadas*, and simple meals. Since most restaurants offer the same menu at both lunch and dinner, the *confitería* is the place to go for a light noon meal. *Porteños* eat a light breakfast, a large lunch between noon and 3 P.M., late-afternoon tea, and a huge late dinner between 10 P.M. and midnight. Restaurants usually stay open until 2 A.M.

RECIPE: BIFE A CABALLO (“BEEF ON HORSEBACK”)

1 beef steak (per person)   Olive oil
1 egg (per person)   Pinch of salt

Coat each steak with olive oil and sprinkle with salt. Grill steak to desired degree of tenderness, preferably on a charcoal grill or barbeque pit. Separately, fry egg sunny side up. When steak is cooked, place egg on top of steak. Serve with mixed salad and crusty bread.

Inside a rural *whiskería,* a bartender chats with his lone customer.

WINE AND OTHER SPIRITS

Argentine wines are considered to be some of the best in South America. Argentina produces its own beer, scotch, rum, and vodka, plus some other liquors, but it exports only wine. The wines of Mendoza are much loved throughout the country. Most Argentines drink red wine with their meals. A highly-prized type is called Malbec. White wines are produced in the Salta region and are also exported.

Chilean wine is also served in many restaurants in Argentina. Wine and champagne coolers mixed with fruit are popular summer drinks. A slightly alcoholic cider called *sidra* ("SEE-drah") is quite popular and often substitutes for champagne on New Year's Eve. *Whiskerías* ("wees-keh-REE-ahs") are numerous in Buenos Aires. These informal cocktail lounges also serve sandwiches. Generally, Argentines tend to chat over coffee or a soft drink rather than cocktails. While they love to drink wine with meals, Argentines also enjoy carbonated mineral water with their food.

YERBA MATE

Mate is a type of tea made from the young leaves of the Brazilian holly, an evergreen tree of the holly family. The tea leaves come both from trees grown on plantations and from trees growing wild in the Misiones jungles. Also known as Paraguayan tea, this drink is commonly called *yerba mate*.

To prepare it, the greenish herb is ground to the size of ordinary tea leaves. The leaves are steeped in very hot water in a gourd or bowl, then drunk from a small hole in the top through a metal straw called a *bombilla* ("bohm-BEE-zhah"). The straw has a filter to keep the leaves out of the drinker's mouth. The bowl and the *bombilla* may be ornately decorated, often with silver. *Yerba mate* was developed by the indigenous Indians, adopted by the *gauchos*, and finally adopted by the entire country. In home parties, *mate* may be served plain or with sugar, anise seeds, orange peel, or milk. The drink is sometimes shared socially, passed around as each person takes a sip from the same cup. Like regular tea, *mate* contains caffeine. In the past, the *gauchos* found that *mate* energized them so much that they could go for long stretches on horseback without food or sleep.

CHIMICHURRI

This is a classic Argentine sauce, often served with grilled beef. This recipe makes one cup of *chimichurri*.

$^1/_2$ cup olive oil
$^1/_4$ cup vinegar
1 cup finely-chopped onion
1 teaspoon finely-chopped or minced parsley
1 teaspoon dry oregano
Salt, freshly ground pepper, and ground chilli peppers, to taste

Combine all ingredients in a bowl and set aside for a few hours until the flavors blend. Serve with cooked meat or use as a marinade before cooking. Ideal for beef.

DULCE DE LECHE

Mostly used as pastry filling, *dulce de leche* can also be enjoyed on bread. This recipe serves ten.

2 quarts (2 liters) milk
1 pound (500 g) sugar
$\frac{1}{2}$ teaspoon bicarbonate of soda
Few drops vanilla flavoring

Heat milk in a pot until it comes to a boil. Remove milk from fire and transfer to a large saucepan. Add sugar, soda, and vanilla and continue to cook on medium heat while stirring with a wooden spoon. Bring mixture to a boil and keep the temperature high. Once it boils, sugar will begin to thicken, so keep stirring to prevent the mixture from sticking to the bottom of the pan. Once mixture has thickened to the consistency of a light cream sauce, remove pan from heat. Cool pan by placing it in a basin filled with cold water. Stir contents until they cool. If mixture separates, blend it until it reforms. Dulce can be refrigerated until served.

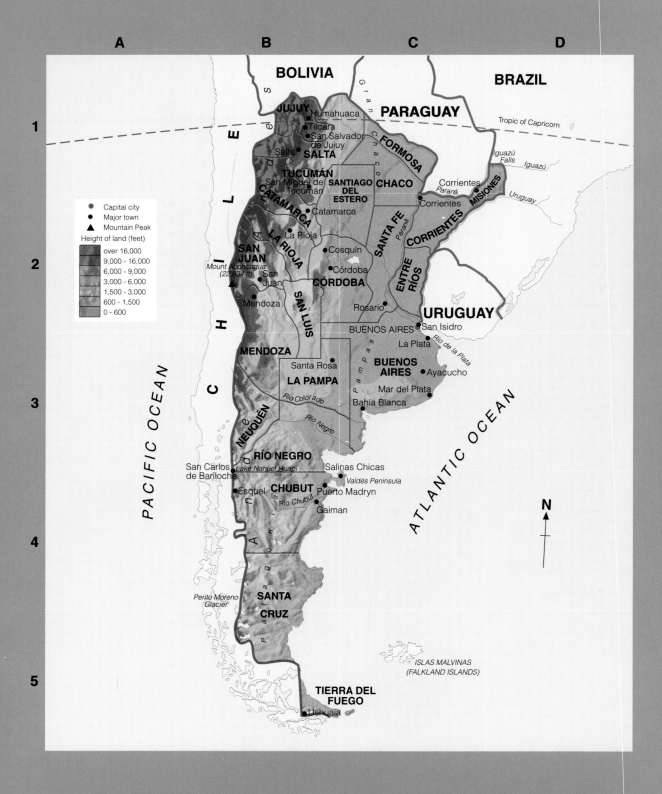

A B C D

1

BOLIVIA   BRAZIL

JUJUY   Humahuaca   PARAGUAY
        Tilcara
        San Salvador   Tropic of Capricorn
        de Jujuy
    Salta   SALTA   Iguazú
                                                Falls   Iguazú
    TUCUMÁN
    San Miguel de   SANTIAGO   CHACO   Corrientes
    Tucumán   CATAMARCA   DEL   Paraná
                ESTERO   Corrientes   MISIONES
        Catamarca
                                            CORRIENTES
    LA RIOJA
    La Rioja   SANTA FE
SAN   Cosquín   ENTRE
JUAN   Mount Aconcagua   Córdoba   RÍOS
    (22,834 ft)   San   CÓRDOBA
        Juan   URUGUAY
    Mendoza   Rosario
                SAN LUIS   BUENOS AIRES   San Isidro
                                            La Plata
MENDOZA   BUENOS   Ayacucho
        Santa Rosa   Pampas   AIRES
                LA PAMPA   Mar del Plata
            Río Colorado   Bahía Blanca

NEUQUÉN   Río Negro
    RÍO NEGRO
San Carlos   Lake Nahuel Huapi   Salinas Chicas
de Bariloche
    Esquel   CHUBUT   Puerto Madryn   Valdés Peninsula
            Río Chubut
        Gaiman

PACIFIC OCEAN   ATLANTIC OCEAN

        SANTA
Perito Moreno   CRUZ
Glacier

                                ISLAS MALVINAS
                                (FALKLAND ISLANDS)

    TIERRA DEL
    FUEGO
        Ushuaia

CHILE

Legend:
● Capital city
● Major town
▲ Mountain Peak

Height of land (feet)
over 16,000
9,000 - 16,000
6,000 - 9,000
3,000 - 6,000
1,500 - 3,000
600 - 1,500
0 - 600

N

MAP OF ARGENTINA

ECONOMIC ARGENTINA

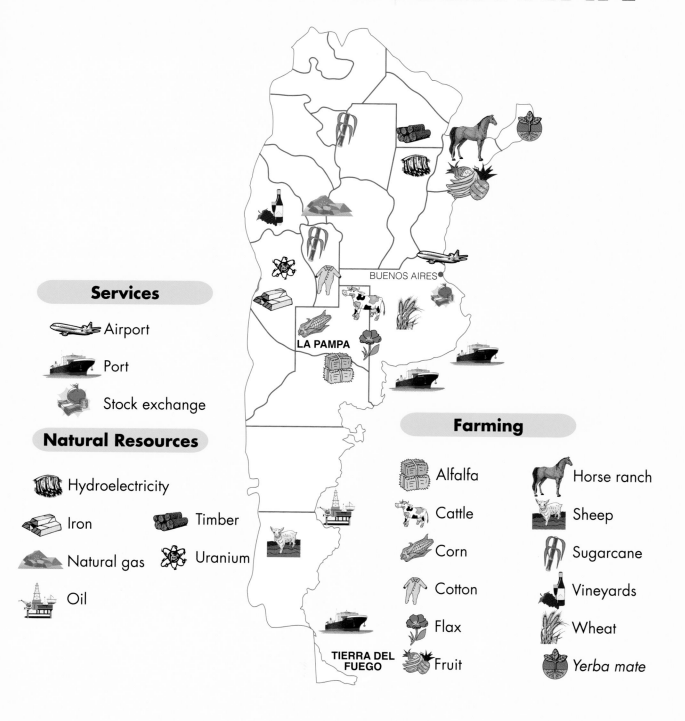

BUENOS AIRES

LA PAMPA

TIERRA DEL FUEGO

Services

- ✈ Airport
- 🚢 Port
- 📈 Stock exchange

Natural Resources

- Hydroelectricity
- Iron
- Natural gas
- Oil
- Timber
- Uranium

Farming

- Alfalfa
- Cattle
- Corn
- Cotton
- Flax
- Fruit
- Horse ranch
- Sheep
- Sugarcane
- Vineyards
- Wheat
- *Yerba mate*

ABOUT THE ECONOMY

OVERVIEW

Argentina's economic strengths lie in its abundant natural resources, highly literate population, and profitable agricultural and industrial exports. The country's high inflation rates of the past decades and a huge external debt slowed the country's economic growth considerably.

Since taking office in 1999, however, the administration of President de la Rúa has made progress in stabilizing the economy by supporting trade liberalization and privatization of state-owned industries.

GDP

$367 billion (1999)

GDP PER CAPITA

$10,000 (1999)

GDP SECTORS

Agriculture: 7 percent
Industry: 29 percent
Services: 64 percent
(1999 estimate)

CURRENCY

1 Peso = 100 centavos
US$1 = 1 peso (the peso is tied to the US Dollar)

WORKFORCE

15 million (1999)

UNEMPLOYMENT RATE

15 percent (2000)

MAIN IMPORTS

Machinery and equipment, motor vehicles, chemicals, metal products, and plastics

MAIN EXPORTS

Edible oils, fuels and energy, cereals, animal feed, and motor vehicles

MAIN TRADING PARTNERS

Brazil, the European Union, and the United States

AGRICULTURAL PRODUCTS

Corn, grapes, lemons, peanuts, soybeans, sunflower seeds, tea, tobacco, and wheat

ENERGY

Fossil fuels: 43 percent
Hydro: 48 percent
Nuclear: 10 percent

TRANSPORTATION

Highways: 133,870 miles (215,434 km) of which 39,492 miles (63,553 km) are paved
Railways: 23,815 miles (38,326 km)
Airports: 1,359 of which 142 have paved runways
Main ports: Bahia Blanca, Buenos Aires, Comodoro Rivadavia, La Plata, Mar del Plata, Necochea, Rio Gallegos, Rosario, Santa Fe, Ushuaia

CULTURAL ARGENTINA

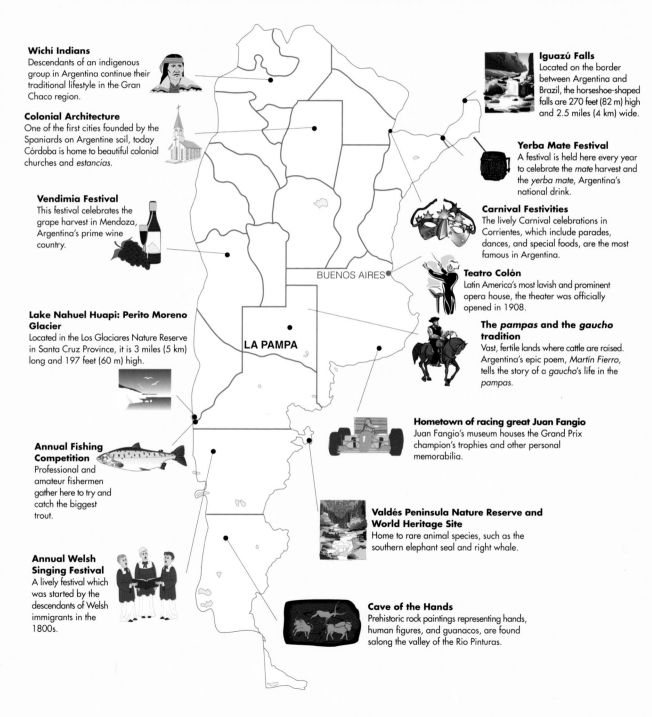

Wichí Indians
Descendants of an indigenous group in Argentina continue their traditional lifestyle in the Gran Chaco region.

Colonial Architecture
One of the first cities founded by the Spaniards on Argentine soil, today Córdoba is home to beautiful colonial churches and *estancias*.

Vendimia Festival
This festival celebrates the grape harvest in Mendoza, Argentina's prime wine country.

Lake Nahuel Huapi: Perito Moreno Glacier
Located in the Los Glaciares Nature Reserve in Santa Cruz Province, it is 3 miles (5 km) long and 197 feet (60 m) high.

Annual Fishing Competition
Professional and amateur fishermen gather here to try and catch the biggest trout.

Annual Welsh Singing Festival
A lively festival which was started by the descendants of Welsh immigrants in the 1800s.

Iguazú Falls
Located on the border between Argentina and Brazil, the horseshoe-shaped falls are 270 feet (82 m) high and 2.5 miles (4 km) wide.

Yerba Mate Festival
A festival is held here every year to celebrate the *mate* harvest and the *yerba mate*, Argentina's national drink.

Carnival Festivities
The lively Carnival celebrations in Corrientes, which include parades, dances, and special foods, are the most famous in Argentina.

Teatro Colón
Latin America's most lavish and prominent opera house, the theater was officially opened in 1908.

The *pampas* and the *gaucho* tradition
Vast, fertile lands where cattle are raised. Argentina's epic poem, *Martín Fierro*, tells the story of a *gaucho*'s life in the *pampas*.

Hometown of racing great Juan Fangio
Juan Fangio's museum houses the Grand Prix champion's trophies and other personal memorabilia.

Valdés Peninsula Nature Reserve and World Heritage Site
Home to rare animal species, such as the southern elephant seal and right whale.

Cave of the Hands
Prehistoric rock paintings representing hands, human figures, and guanacos, are found salong the valley of the Rio Pinturas.

BUENOS AIRES

LA PAMPA

ABOUT THE CULTURE

OFFICIAL NAME
República Argentina, or Republic of Argentina

CAPITAL
Buenos Aires

DESCRIPTION OF FLAG
Three horizontal bands of light blue, white, and light blue with a radiant sun, known as the Sun of May, in the middle of the white band.

NATIONAL ANTHEM
Oid mortales el grito sagrado ("Listen, o mortals, the sacred cry")

POLITICS
Fernando de la Rua, president since 1999
Voting age: 18
Constitution: Established May 1853, last revised August 1994

POPULATION
37 million (2000)
Birth rate: 18.6 births per 1,000 people
Infant mortality rate: 18.3 deaths per 1,000 births
Fertility rate: 2.5 children per woman

LIFE EXPECTANCY
Male: 72
Female: 79

ETHNIC GROUPS
Caucasian: 85 percent
Mestizo, Amerindian, and others: 15 percent

LITERACY RATE
Total population: 96 percent
Male: 96 percent
Female: 96 percent

NATIONAL HOLIDAYS
Jan. 1—New Year's Day; Jan. 6—Epiphany; Mar./Apr.—Maundy Thursday, Good Friday, Easter Sunday; May 1—Labor Day; May 25—Anniversary of Revolution of 1810; Jun. 10—Malvinas Day; Jun. 20—Flag Day; Jul. 9—Independence Day; Aug. 17—Death of General José de San Martín; Oct. 12—Colombus Day; Dec. 8—Immaculate Conception; Dec. 25—Christmas.

LEADERS IN SPORTS
Diego Armando Maradona, soccer player; Gabriel Batistuta, soccer player; Guillermo Vilas, tennis player; Gabriela Sabatini, tennis player; Franco Squillari, tennis player.

LEADERS IN THE ARTS
Jorge Luis Borges, writer; Carlos Gardel, tango singer; Astor Piazzolla, tango musician; Benito Quinquela, painter; Norma Aleandro, actress.

TIME LINE

IN ARGENTINA	IN THE WORLD

7,370 B.C.
First hand paintings made at the Cave of the
Hands in Santa Cruz province

753 B.C.
Rome founded

34 B.C.
Death of Plato, Ancient Greek philosopher

116–17 B.C.
Roman Empire reaches its greatest extent, under
Emperor Trajan (98-17)

600 A.D.
Height of Mayan civilization

1000
Chinese perfect gunpowder and begin to use it
in warfare

1440–68
Reign of Aztec emperor Moctezuma I

1516
Juan Díaz de Solís claims
Rio de la Plata for Spain.

1527
Sebastian Cabot founds the first European
settlement near Rosario.

1530
Beginning of trans-Atlantic slave trade organized
by Portuguese in Africa

1536
First founding of Santa María del Buen Aire

1580
Founding of Buenos Aires after failed attempts

1558–1603
Reign of Elizabeth I of England

1620
Pilgrim Fathers sail the Mayflower to America

1681
Frenchman LaSalle explores Mississippi river
from source to mouth, and founds Louisiana

1776
Spanish Crown establishes
the Viceroyalty of Rio de la Plata.

1776
U. S. Declaration of Independence

1789–1799
The French Revolution

1806–1807
Great Britain attempts to invade Buenos Aires.

1810
Rio de la Plata declares
its independence from Spain.

IN ARGENTINA	IN THE WORLD
1816 Formal declaration of independence in Tucumán	
1828–1829 Civil war.	
1853–1854 New constitution is created.	
1860 The country's name is changed to Argentina.	
	1861 U. S. Civil War begins.
	1869 The Suez Canal is opened.
1890–1914 Golden Age of economic expansion	**1914** World War I begins.
1944 Perón becomes vice-president.	**1939** World War II begins.
1945 Argentina declares war on Germany and Japan.	**1945** The United States drops atomic bombs on Hiroshima and Nagasaki.
1946 Perón becomes president.	**1949** North Atlantic Treaty Organization (NATO) formed
	1957 Russians launch Sputnik.
	1966–1969 Chinese Cultural Revolution
1976–1983 The Dirty War	
1983 Democratic government returns; Raúl Alfonsín becomes president.	**1986** Nuclear power disaster at Chernobyl in Ukraine
	1991 Break-up of Soviet Union
	1997 Hong Kong is returned to China.
1999 Fernando de la Rúa is elected president.	**2001** World population surpasses 6 billion.

GLOSSARY

bandoneón ("bahn-doh-NYOHN")
An instrument similar to the accordion, often used when performing the tango.

campesino ("kam-peh-SEE-noh")
A person who lives in the countryside.

confitería ("kohn-fee-teh-REE-ah")
A casual eatery found only in Argentina that serves coffee, tea, pastries, and light meals.

criollo ("kree-OH-yoh")
A person of Spanish descent born in Latin America.

estancia ("es-TAHN-see-ah")
A large cattle ranch.

fiestas ("fee-EHS-tahs")
Festivities linked to special holidays.

gaucho ("GOW-choh")
A horseman and cowboy of the pampas, usually a mestizo.

lunfardo ("loon-FAR-doh")
A slang language, originally used by the criminals of Buenos Aires. It is used in tango music, popular songs, poetry, and the theater.

mestizo ("mess-TEE-soh")
A person of mixed European and Indian ancestry.

pampas ("PAHM-pahs")
The flat grass plains of central Argentina.

parrillada ("par-ree-ZHAH-dah")
A restaurant which specializes in serving beef and other meats grilled over a charcoal fire.

pato ("PAH-toh")
A sport played on horseback, in which players attempt to throw a six-handled leather ball into a net at the opposing team's end of the playing field.

peninsulares ("pay-neen-soo-LAH-rehs")
Spaniards who occupied all high government positions in the Latin American colonies.

piropo ("pee-ROH-poh")
A casual comment made by a man to attract a woman's attention as she passes by.

porteños ("porr-TEH-nyos")
The people of the city of Buenos Aires.

tango ("TAHN-goh")
A dance, accompanied by music, in which a couple hold each other and take long, gliding steps together, occasionally pausing in a dramatic pose.

yerba mate ("ZHER-bah MAH-teh")
A holly tea sipped from a gourd through a metal straw.

FURTHER INFORMATION

BOOKS

Azzi, Maria Susana and Simon Collier. *Le Grand Tango: The Life and Music of Astor Piazzolla.* Oxford: Oxford University Press, 2000.

Brooks, Shirley Lomax. *Argentina Cooks: Treasured Recipes From the Nine Regions of Argentina.* Hippocrane Books, 2001.

Dalal, Anita. *Argentina.* Nations of the World series. Austin: Raintree Steck-Vaughn, 2000.

Egan, E.W. *Argentina in Pictures.* Minneapolis: Lerner Publications, 1999.

Kent, Deborah. *Buenos Aires.* Cities of the World series. Chicago: Children's Press, 1998.

Nickels, Greg and Bobbie Kalman. *Argentina: The Land.* Ontario: Crabtree Press, 2000.

Nickels, Greg and Bobbie Kalman. *Argentina: The People.* Ontario: Crabtree Press, 2000.

Shaw, Edward. *At Home in Buenos Aires.* New York: Abbeville Press, 1999.

WEBSITES

abcTango. www.abctango.com.ar/english/indexi.html

Central Intelligence Agency World Factbook (select "Argentina" from the country list). www.odci.gov/cia/publications/factbook/index.html

Diego Maradona Official Site. www.diegomaradona.com

Lonely Planet World Guide: Destination Argentina. www.lonelyplanet.com/destinations/south_america/argentina

Ministry of Tourism of Argentina. www.sectur.gov.ar/eng/menu.htm

The Vanished Gallery: The Desaparecidos of Argentina. www.yendor.com/vanished

MUSIC

Bailemos Tango: A Century of Tango on the Dance Floor. Rhino Records, 2000.

VIDEOS

Evita. Buena Vista Home Entertainment, 1996.

On Top of the World: Argentina. Superior Home Video, 1994.

BIBLIOGRAPHY

Argentina in Pictures, Lerner Publications Company, Minneapolis, 1988.

Fox, Geoffrey E., *The Land and People of Argentina*, Lippencott, New York, 1990.

Hernández, José, *The Gaucho Martin Fierro*, Editorial Pampa, Buenos Aires, 1960. Adapted from the Spanish and rendered into English verse by Walter Owen with drawings by Alberto Guiraldez.

Hintz, Martin, *Argentina*, Chicago Children's Press, Chicago, 1985.

Huber, Alex, *We Live in Argentina*, The Bookwright Press, New York, 1984.

INDEX

98·38